Delphine Horvilleur is one of the few female rabbis in France. She was ordained in America, as there was no possibility for women to study in France, and is the leader of the Liberal Jewish Movement of France. Her writing has appeared in the *Washington Post*, *Le Monde*, and *Haaretz*, among others. She lives in Paris.

Lisa Appignanesi is the author of several critically acclaimed and prizewinning books on the history of madness and mind-doctoring, most recently *Everyday Madness: On Grief, Anger, Loss and Love*. She has written for the *New York Review of Books*, the *Guardian*, and the *Observer*. She is a former President of English PEN, chair of the Freud Museum, London, and the Royal Society of Literature.

HOW ISN'T IT GOING?

ALSO BY

DELPHINE HORVILLEUR

Living with Our Dead

Delphine Horvilleur

HOW ISN'T IT GOING?

Conversations after October 7

Translated from the French
by Lisa Appignanesi

Europa Editions
27 Union Square West, Suite 302
New York NY 10003
www.europaeditions.com
info@europaeditions.com

First publication 2025 by Europa Editions

Translation by Lisa Appignanesi
Original title: *Comment ça va pas?*

Library of Congress Cataloging in Publication Data is available
ISBN 979-8-88966-060-6

Horvilleur, Delphine
How Isn't It Going?

Cover design and illustration by Ginevra Rapisardi

Prepress by Grafica Punto Print – Rome

Printed in the USA

CONTENTS

As you prepare your breakfast, think of others
(do not forget the pigeon's food).
As you conduct your wars, think of others
(do not forget those who seek peace).
As you pay your water bill, think of others
(those who are nursed by clouds).
As you return home, to your home, think of others
(do not forget the people of the camps).
As you sleep and count the stars, think of others
(those who have nowhere to sleep).
As you liberate yourself in metaphor, think of others
(those who have lost the right to speak).
As you think of others far away, think of yourself
(say: "If only I were a candle in the dark").

—Mahmoud Darwish, *Think of Others*[1]

[1] "Think of Others" by Mahmoud Darwish, from *Almond Blossoms and Beyond*. Translated from the original Arabic by Mohammed Shaheen. Interlink Books, 2010.

À mes enfants Samuel, Ella et Alma . . .
Et à tous les autres, ces “Mensch” en devenir qui
à Paris, Tel-Aviv, Gaza ou ailleurs . . .
se relèveront de la haine et sauront être
des bougies dans le noir.

To my children Samuel, Ella, and Alma
And to all the other “mensch” to come
In Paris, Tel-Aviv, Gaza, and elsewhere
Who will emerge from hatred
And illuminate the darkness

HOW ISN'T IT GOING?

1
Conversation with my Pain

"Oy a broch!"

In my childhood, conversations often started with this phrase.

An adult came into the room—parent, grandparent, or friend of the family. They looked us straight in the eyes and with a great sigh, murmured the magic formula: "*Oy a broch!*" "What a curse!"

These three words can equally imply, "What a shit of a day!" or "Things aren't so bad, but beware . . . it won't last." They could mean, "How sweet you are, children" or "Hmm . . . One day you'll be old fools, too!"

Everything depends on context.

There were variations on the expression, subtle alternatives of the classic formulation: "*Oy vay,*" "*Oy vavoy.*" "*Oy vay iz mir,*" literally, "Woe is me." But no matter how this phrase was pronounced, it always mixed despair and humor, an awareness of the drama at hand and a way of mocking it. The phrases constituted what in Yiddish is known as *krekhts*, a word meaning "moan" that's hard to pronounce since it scrapes the throat and almost has you spitting. But it's milder than it seems. It designates that very Jewish capacity of knowing how to complain *with humor*. It carries the power of a sob that explodes into laughter.

My childhood ear recognized the melody perfectly. It resonated like Klezmer music and held a very particular promise. It stated, in that mysterious language, that we were forever linked to our history. The syllables carried old legends, transmitted almost religiously from one generation to the next: the consciousness of misfortune and the duty to survive it, the memory of tragedies and the refusal to let yourself be told by them.

"Listen my child," the words said, "here's what happened to us, but we are not only what has happened to us . . . We are what we will make of it, *keyne hore*![2] . . . Now have a little more chicken soup."

"*Oy a broch*! [. . .]"

Even as a child, I knew that it wasn't necessary to translate these words to understand them. Their literal sense made no real difference. "What a curse!" "Woe betide me!" Beyond their actual meaning, lay a secret message concealed by my ancestors: a stash of words in a language that wasn't really one.

Specialists recognize it now: Yiddish is not a structured language, but a sort of protean patois, a jargon

[2] *Keyne hore* "without the evil eye" or "the evil eye permitting": this is an expression uttered each time one fears that the envy of another might bring us bad luck.

built out of High German but also the Slavic languages and Hebrew. A powerful linguistic glue, it carries with it the residue of a desperate migration. It bears the traces of all the places from which we were thrown out, half alive or almost completely massacred. It's the language of those who take care, in leaving a place, to pick up all the crumbs of words they can chew on as they travel.

That's how the language of the wandering person works: it won't stand for a single reliable translation that would install it once and for all in a dictionary. All attempts to make it adhere to some place, even to a lexicon, are in vain because it wanders off, just like the person who speaks it.

The official translators of Yiddish, even the most attentive or erudite ones, always fail. They just miss the point and finally have to give up on finding an exact definition, literal or metaphoric, having created another flop. The nuances of Yiddish always create a "not quite right." They won't allow themselves either to be completely captured or wholly understood. This is true of all the words, but most true of the insults, the absolute treasure of my people. The greatest riches lie hidden in swear words—desperate jewels that you throw into the face of the enemy, knowing full well that he can't recover from them. Even if he's in the process of exterminating you.

Such words do nothing to alter your impotence or vulnerability, of course, but because they give you the opportunity of laughter, they make you into an invincible adversary. Thus, in Yiddish, there are a thousand expressions with which to damn your enemy and even more with which to wish the worst of catastrophes on him. "*Altekaker*, you old shitbag, may you lose all your teeth . . . all but one, as long as that one is full of cavities."

"*Oy a broch.*"

To my childhood ears, these three words aroused a strange sense of belonging. Not to Judaism, about which I didn't care much, nor to a tribe or a religious group, but to a sort of human brotherhood, an international confederation of down and outs. Whatever happened, I could always be tied to them.

With this as a rallying cry, a strange barefoot regiment mobilized around me—an army united across time and space, all those who went about on an empty stomach. All those whom history, in its great bowling game, took pains to fell at regular intervals. Those on whom, time and again, the senseless wrath of a world determined never to spare them would fall.

As a child, I liked the idea of all that Yiddish carried of our past grandeur. The loser's heritage offered a certain pedigree. It also gave us a capacity to laugh in that language about all that had happened us.

As I grew up, of course, I learned to speak other languages—more solid ones, the languages of conquerors. And I let my Yiddish fall dormant.

I felt sufficiently secure. I convinced myself that all

those bad things wouldn't happen to us again. I imagined that for my generation, protected from threats, this language would be less pertinent, less meaningful. The lamenting trumpets of "*Oy a broch*" would stay silent, or almost. And if that were the case, my children wouldn't hear their sounds at all.

In short, I told myself fairy tales.

Do you know this one? It's the story of two Jews who had been through lots of trials and tribulations together. Then life separated them. They lost sight of each other for decades. Then miraculously, one day by pure chance they bumped into each other.

The first said: "I'm so very happy to see you again, Moshe. But tell me, how have you been getting on? How are you?"

Without thinking, Moshe says, "Fine!"

"But seriously, Moshe, tell me more: how are you? In two words . . ."

Moshe cuts him off. "In two words? . . . Not fine."

Fine . . . Not fine. This story is obviously mine. Since October 7, 2023, I am Moshe. I and a lot of others, all of us laid low. Every day our paths cross, but it's as if we had lost sight of each other. I meet men and women with whom I don't really know how to engage in conversation. It's strange, but it's as if the language of the everyday has ceased to function; I walk into a room and the habitual codes, the rules of ordinary protocol for discussion, seem to be malfunctioning. I'm asked: "How is it going?"

I know that my interlocutor through this banal question means me no harm, and sometimes, only good. He interrogates me with good intentions or naively. He's trying to establish a link, without noticing the acuteness of my pain.

"Fine," I respond . . . And then I say, "Not fine."

Sometimes I speak to both replies, using the old codes of the Jewish tradition—that well-known method which suggests that to avoid questions, it's always good to respond to one question with another. When asked, "How's it going?," I say "And with you? Don't you think it's rather dry for November? What time is it?"

Sometimes, when nothing works, I remember the obscure origins of this daily expression—"How are you?" or "How's it going?" In the Middle Ages, people asked each other, "How are your bowel movements?" Here lay a principal indicator of one's state of health: the consistency, the frequency, the smell of your stool. Our "How's it going?" is a sanitized abbreviation, the lexical residue of a physiological question. In short, a shitty question.

Since October 7, I carefully avoid answering it. I rid myself of all the rules of politeness.

I wish that all conversational codes could suddenly change, that all human encounters with near ones or strangers took place in other formulations. I dream that we might even invent another language. Or better still, I dream that the entire world understood that from now on nothing is said except in Yiddish.

Whether we are Jewish or not, pro-Israeli, pro-Palestinian, pro-foundly tired or just pro-strate in our grief, what matter! Those of us who are devastated, who in our words and in our lives drag around the sufferings of our histories, can no longer really speak only in our ordinary languages. I would so love it if, each time we bumped into each other, we could just say, "*Oy a broch*"—a greeting that rings true when our stomachs are wracked by pain and our guts in turmoil.

"*Oy a broch, Sir.*"
"*Oy a broch, Ms.*"
"*Oy vay is mir*, what can I get for you today?"
"*Oy vay*—a small espresso, as usual, thank you."

Since the seventh of October 2023, wherever we find ourselves, whoever our interlocutors might be, and whatever situation we face, all languages need to be spoken in Yiddish. Make no mistake: Yiddish isn't the language of Jews. It's the language of all people who see from the depths of despair that their shaky humanity calls out to be saved.

2
Conversation with my Grandparents

"*Oy a broch*, Gramps . . ."

"But my big little granddaughter (that's always the way he addressed me in serious conversations), you mustn't speak that way."

"Speak how, Gramps?"

"Speak in Yiddish. You need to speak French. Only French."

Speak French. My paternal grandfather did that better than anyone else. It was his profession and his passion. A graduate in Classics, he taught literature, Latin and Greek. Above all, he venerated grammar. He corrected my schoolwork, my translations, and essays. Often, he annotated my assignments, even when I didn't ask him to. Especially when I didn't ask him to. He would get a red pencil and underline my mistakes, correct my style, write notes in the margins.

It took me a while to understand that this very modest man, restrained in manifestations of feeling and economic in his tender gestures, showed his emotion with a red pencil. Crossed-out copy was a declaration of love, corrected stylistic points were equivalent to hugs. Through a reflexive verb, I felt myself loved. A coordinating conjunction made that definite.

He was as deft with rules of grammar as he was clumsy with relational intelligence. And so he hid the sobs I wouldn't know how to see.

One day, for example, having read Elie Wiesel's *Night*, I wrote my grandfather a brief message. I needed to share my emotion with him and tell him how shaken I was by Wiesel's harrowing account of deportation and life in the Nazi camps. The next day I received a long letter in reply from him, in which he told me in emphatic fashion that "*génocide*" was written with an acute accent and not with a circumflex. I recognized his meaning. It held an intense expression of love. We were at the apogee of emotion. For a long time, I kept this precious message, folded in my handbag. I carried it everywhere and reread it regularly, anytime I was on the brink of losing control of my emotions. I was then able to remember that if "*génocide*" took an acute accent, "*gênance*," embarrassment, always kept its circumflex. It was figuratively hemmed round. With these words, I had the formal proof that my grandfather loved me as much as he did French. And that was no small matter.

The French language was his greatest love, the symbol of his immense gratitude to France. He owed to the Republic his education and his passion, and above all his saved life. It had given him the opportunity of false papers and of encountering the path of the Just. Thus, he had survived the war, thanks to a borrowed name and a surprising means of employment.

He, the great intellectual incapable of changing a lightbulb or hammering a nail, a cerebral man of minimal emotion and repressed affection, had in hiding been a lockkeeper. The man who knew so well how to block his own tear channels, keep the dikes of emotion hermetically sealed, under his borrowed name had overseen the river canals, allowing water to flow and ships to cross by activating cranks.

I often think of this other grandfather, the clandestine lockkeeper. I had, of course, never known the mysterious double he was during the war. I sometimes wonder whether that man committed spelling mistakes. Did he ever fail to make his past participles agree? Did he ever give a huge hug to those he loved?

When my grandfather talked of the glorious France of the Resistance, he offered up a narrative of eternal gratitude. In the process he became the perfect French Jew, onesome of those who until recently were called "*Israelites.*" The *Israelite* is a patriot for whom Jewishness is a matter of extreme discretion and of altogether private practice. My grandfather was like those Spanish Marranos forced to convert by the Inquisition from Judaism to Christianity: he was a perfectly assimilated Jew of a kind that no longer exists.

Some would say that's a pity. Personally, I'm not so sure. The Jewish practices of that generation, so discreet as to be practically invisible, undoubtedly contained a profound uneasiness, a fear of never being the altogether legitimate spouse of the adored country, of forever remaining the secret mistress—the one who sooner or later is inevitably repudiated so that hearth and home can be protected. His debt to the nation harboured this existential doubt. Extreme gratitude was the flamboyant cloak that elegantly veiled those very Jewish anxieties and sufferings: the fear of not being loved as much as one loves.

"*Oy a broch*, Gramps."

"No, no, no, my big little granddaughter. Don't speak in Yiddish. There are enough words in French to describe your pain or your solitude precisely. All you have to do is choose them well. Out of these thousands of words, masterpieces have been created. You know that because we've often read long theatre speeches together. Remember your Racine and Corneille, the power of classical theatre, the force of the great tragedies."

"You're right, Gramps. Thanks to you I know all those speeches and poems in Alexandrines by heart, all those verses and universal dramas. I know how to declaim with great panache the sufferings of others . . . and through them prevent ours from appearing too blatant. Listen, Gramps, to how well I remember my Corneille:

'Rome, unique object of my resentment!
Rome whose arm has just imprisoned my lover!
Rome who saw you born and which your heart adores!

Rome, which I loathe, because it honors you!'"

"Bravo, my big granddaughter. You haven't forgotten Camille who in *Horace* weeps because she has been betrayed by her own, by her brother who has murdered her love and doesn't know how to protect her."

"Yes, Gramps, it's a magnificent play. But tell me: if a brother, a near one, or even a country one loves, doesn't know how to protect us, or worse, sends us off to death, is it still worthy of our love and our confidence. Does it still really merit our respect? Are you listening, Gramps?"

He didn't have time to answer me because it was at that very moment that *She* leapt into my mind.

"*Maidele*, my little doll. (She never called me by that name—which means little girl in Yiddish, but I would have loved to have been called that!) *Maidele*, what are these French Tragedy idiocies???"

She appeared before me right in the midst of this imaginary conversation. Her voice resounded and I had to listen to her.

When she was alive, she would never have broken in. She would neither interrupt a conversation, nor talk loudly, certainly not to comment on Corneille's text. My grandmother had never read him, nor Racine or Molière, and I don't know what she was doing in this company. But here she was and talking very loudly.

In my memory, while she was alive, she never spoke loudly. In fact, she rarely spoke at all. She kept her thoughts to herself. Or more precisely, everything she said was uttered in silence and in Yiddish. Her absolute mutism only found expression in this language of survivors: because wherever they come from and whatever their history is, this is their most obvious means of expression.

Interrupting my conversation with Gramps, it seems to me that she said in her heavy accent from the Carpathian mountains:

"What are these idiocies? *Genuk azoy* . . . Enough already with Corneille and your Molière and all these *shmucks*, these male nincompoops. What do they know of tragedy? What exactly did they undergo these little *pishers*, those brats? And these old geysers, these *Altekackers*, who think they're going to give us lessons in tragedy! Us! *Gay avek.* Get out of here!"

I had never seen my Granny so agitated. She had died so long ago, but for a ghost she had really come up well. It's clear the expression "rest in peace" makes no sense. Why shouldn't the dead have the right to get agitated!

When she was alive, my Granny didn't engage in harangues or anger—or else she hid it well. She always seemed absent or extinguished. Maybe she was getting her revenge now, in the never-never.

As a child I knew nothing about her past. I guessed that a catastrophe had rendered her mute. I knew that any questions about this were forbidden.

First, because I didn't want to give anyone pain—I already suspected that talking might awaken pain that was impossible to master. There was no question of unleashing a family tsunami. On top of that, I didn't want to nullify the efforts of the adults. They seemed so busy building ramparts, putting dykes and dams in place to protect us and to try to prevent a hurricane of memories from sweeping away my generation. I could see that this was a fulltime job, and the construction site was enormous. I didn't want them to exhaust themselves in the task. We had to help them, at least a little.

Finally, I had understood very young that in my family, everyone held the same profession. We were all lockkeepers, from father to son, mother to daughter, everyone in their own fashion. Whether our papers were genuine or forged, whether we used words or not, we all tried to build fortifications as best we could, even though we knew they wouldn't stand up. No chance of that.

So now grandma appeared in our conversation with her uncertain French, heavily accented with Eastern European, the kind of speech that transposes all the vowels randomly for one another. She said: "*Maidele*, why you look for answers in French books. To what end?"

She really believed in the necessity of having a goal in life, even if to tell the truth I never knew what hers was. Mine, when she addressed me in her thick accents, was not to burst into giggles. In listening to her, I tried everything not to erupt in mad laugher, the kind that grips you when you're on the verge of tears. Above all, I didn't want her to think that I was mocking her. I held my lips hermetically sealed.

"So, tell me, what's your goal?"

I didn't say anything. That's when she would turn to Gramps and ask him in her strange inarticulate French.

"Mister, this Fronce you like so much, full of beautiful books and culture, the Fronce of Victor Hugo and Albert Camus, it don't like Jews any more than they were liked where I was born. What you think? Grammar is goin' to save you?"

That's when I understood that this conversation between my dead grandparents held a really jarring note. It was embarrassing, as my children now say. (Not that my children were born at the time when my grandparents might have had this conversation in my presence, a conversation they would in fact never have engaged in with or without me, even if that were technically possible. *Oy vay*, what an intergenerational muddle!)

My French, Jewish grandfather saved during the war by non-Jews, and my stateless Jewish grandmother not at all saved by non-Jews . . . would never have spoken to each other in this way. Lots of things went into the silencing—whether polite or resigned—of the conversation they never really had with each other: class contempt; the lack of common vocabulary; above all, too much that was unspeakable. They couldn't find words to put to their sufferings.

Alive, they never really spoke to one another. So, let's be clear: if they speak in these pages now that they're long dead, it's only because absent ones are always chattier than the living. Ghosts have dating sites too, especially if, when they were alive, they failed to speak much. And it's even truer that when History pings, they answer the call. It goes without saying that on October 7, History sent them a sacred convocation. It summoned them to turn up and, of course, they both landed in my head.

3
Conversation with Jewish Paranoia

Since October 7, 2023, around me the world has filled with people who have more or less the same conversation as mine with their parents or with their (dead) grandparents. Dialogues with past generations, conscious or repressed, multiply. They come to mind or dream, in synagogues or on the therapist's couch. Like parasites, they creep into our thoughts during the day or haunt our nightmares when we sleep. And in my work, I spend a huge amount of time listening to narratives that echo one another with a residue of inherited trauma.

"Rabbi, I need to speak to you," they say to me.

"My father/grandfather always said to me: 'It'll come back. Don't imagine you're safe from catastrophe.' Of course I never believed him. Do you think that maybe, actually, he was right?"

Or they say:

"My mother/grandmother always said to me: 'Don't worry, the world has understood now: you're safe.' Do you think she was lying? Do you think she was wrong?"

I listen to hundreds of people evoking their fears, their anxieties, or retracing improbable conversations. Sometimes they have them with their own children:

"I knock at the door of his room, and I say: take that star of David straight off your pendant, you hear me? And um . . . dinner will be ready in ten minutes."

Sometimes the conversations are less personal but equally surreal:

"The police knock at the door of my apartment, and they say: 'O.K., could you hurry up and take down that Mezuzah hanging there? And if not, could you perhaps change the name on your mailbox? It won't take more than ten minutes and it would reassure your neighbours.'"

I listen and I shut out my own conversations, those I have with my children, happily alive, and with my grandparents, altogether dead. I don't tell anyone about the police visit to my house, nor their suggestion that I use a pseudonym to book a taxi or a restaurant table. I don't mention our family game with the children which consists in making lists of all the grotesque names we could use to book a holiday or order something online. Often, we adapt the names of writers or actors. These last weeks I was Sylvia Stallone in a taxi and Joanna Wayne at a Japanese restaurant. Our preferences are for American stars, particularly those in a position to either save the planet or destroy it altogether. Because, as everybody knows, in certain milieus, Jews are INCREDIBLY powerful . . . They run the financial world, the media, and especially Hollywood. So, I don't see why one should aim for second-rate pseudonyms. If I could, I would sign this book with a pseudonym: Superman? Batman? Spiderman? No, all those suffixes sound too Jewish. I'm going to aim for something a little more neutral.

I think of that famous Jewish joke about Mr. Katzman who, at all costs, wants to change his name to protect his family and sound less Jewish. He goes off to the registry to Frenchify his family name. The employee suggests he translates Katz "*chat*" (cat) and man by "*homme.*" Mr. Katzman is very relieved: from now on he is to be called, Mr. Chalom.

I don't tell this joke to the people who come and see me, any more than I recount my own anxieties. I don't tell them how paranoid I've become, nor how I've ended up seeing "Jews" everywhere. Not Jewish people, but just the word "Jew." Since October 7, I've been suffering from this strange hallucination, both visual and auditory. It worries me. I see the word Jew everywhere and I hear it often in conversations, even when it's not being used.

Sometimes in the street, it surfaces from nowhere. It only takes people talking about "juice," or "jewels" or "jubilation." Startled, I go closer to listen. I'd bet my arm that they've said the word "Jew." I concentrate to hear better. My ears are so strained that I'll surely end up resembling one of those anti-Semitic cartoons in which Jews have big ears, big noses, and hooked fingers.

My paranoia stretches further. In newspapers, books, on billboards, anywhere in my field of vision, I note everything that resembles the key word. If I see Journal or juggler or JuJu Jerky, I jump. And on each occasion, it takes me a few seconds to reassure myself and soothe my anxiety.

It's ridiculous, I know. But I'm hardly the only one to suffer from this hallucinatory pathology. Friends, too, talk to me about it. And I know that in the past, many generations manifested the same symptoms—authors, intellectuals, poets. The Swiss French-language novelist Albert Cohen, for example, talks about it in his autobiography, *O Humans, My Brothers.* He remembers his tenth birthday when a hawker in a street market called him "dirty Jew." Cohen charts the impact of this insult on his life:

"*Since the day of that incident, I could no longer look at a newspaper without immediately, at the very first glance, finding the word that described me. I even spotted the word that resembled the terrible word, painful and beautiful as it is. I immediately saw 'juif' and 'suif' in French, and in English few, dew, jewel. Enough.*"

Cohen wrote "enough," but he knew very well that it wouldn't stop. Neither for him, nor for others. This hallucinatory paranoia comes back into our lives time and again. It'll come back because what unleashes it will never vanish. It speaks of fear and the awareness of threat. The world doesn't understand, I know. Taking in these lines, most of my readers, even the best intentioned, will say, "But what a grotesque pathology. You really have to relax."

Those who haven't inherited this fear can't understand either what it summons up or what it provokes. Those who think that words are only words, who don't understand that they can kill; those who can't imagine that an exclamation of "dirty Jew!" shouted in a crowded market can put in motion a killing machine; these people won't understand. They'll be able to relax. As for us? I doubt it.

These days I notice this incomprehension everywhere around me. Sometimes it's right there in our very living rooms or bedrooms. In these last weeks, it's been narrated to me often in my encounters, by the very people who are living it:

"Rabbi, I need to talk to you. Things aren't going at all well with my husband/my wife (whichever) . . . I'm astonished that he/she doesn't understand my fear. Why is he/she saying that I exaggerate? Why does he/she think I'm paranoid?"

These conjugal crises are hardly new, but suddenly they intimately affect mixed couples. The Jewish spouse in a couple will knock at my door, or the non-Jewish partner who wants to understand what their other half is going through, and I hear them say how very much Jewishness is at the heart of the crisis they are going through. Up until now, they hardly felt Jewish; they didn't go to the synagogue, didn't belong to any community. Or they thought their partner's Jewishness was largely anecdotal, believing that, after all, they weren't as Jewish as all that . . . But all of them speak in phrases where the "Jew" seems present everywhere . . . "I would never have judged it judicious to justify myself . . ." It rings in my ears.

So there you are. The observation is straightforward and clear: Fear has awoken along with all our phantoms. It haunts our conversations with the living and with the dead. It speaks with near ones and total strangers. And as always in History, the world around us says, "Stop dramatizing the situation. Pay attention. It's your trauma speaking. Don't exaggerate the real. Calm down. All will be well."

People want to reassure us. It's good of them. Very good. And we really want to believe them. We want to huddle in their arms and know we will be protected. But the conversation with the past is so powerful, it makes it difficult to hear other things. And in our minds, there's a monstrous din. We're forced to revisit all the narratives that shaped us. We have to deconstruct family legends, the narratives in whose shadow we sheltered for so long.

Take me, for instance. I thought I was more or less clear on my parents' history. I thought I had a precise vision of it all: I held all the cards in hand, like in Seven Families—that old French children's card game.

My father's family were secular republican Jews. What about the grandparents? Got them. They're all in place: not deported, well integrated, proud of their history. Saved in wartime by the "Righteous Among the Nations" and extremely indebted to non-Jews who risked their lives for them.

I look at the cards in my hand and rejoice.

But in my mother's family, they're immigrants from the Carpathian Mountains. Propelled by genocide, they ended up by pure chance in France. There are no parents nor children here. They all went up in smoke in the chimneys of the holocaust. I ask for a set of grandparents. "Hello . . . Is there anyone there?" No response. Of course! That's always the way they manifest themselves.

Silence. Silence about what actually happened to them. Silence about the dead. And silence about the high dose anti-depressants they take to numb the memory. So suspicion reigns forever. But how could it be otherwise? Who can believe the words of non-Jews, those who denounced and assassinated? Who could trust them again?

I skip my turn.

In this strange game of Seven Families, the child I was quickly understood that around the table the sides didn't follow the same rules. On my Gramps' side, there was a lot of heart and trust in others—in a neighbour or a stranger, who was ready to take risks for you.

In my grandmother's hand, there were only spades! And too many cards were missing, so there was no hope of finishing the set. Each card held an awareness of permanent fear: of neighbour, a familiar or a stranger . . . The one you trusted could very well turn on you and exterminate you tomorrow.

Very young, I understood that I had a loaded hand. Some cards said, "trust often" and others "be suspicious all the time." So, I did what I could to invent my own rules.

I always knew that I was growing up in the shadow of conflicting histories. I was riding two irreconcilable stories. On the fault-line between these two worlds, I tried to find my place. I looked for ballast which would allow me not to betray one or the other.

Now I understand that during all those years, I tried to do everything in my power to make the first voice the more resonant one, so as to allow trust to prevail over despair.

I built bridges, and also opened sluices. I wrote books, held speeches that were accessible to everyone. I made of my world, including my Judaism, the site of all possible encounters, a fertile loam for dialogue with others.

But . . . For several weeks now, my grandmother has surfaced in me with a new strength. In my card game of Seven Families, she now holds the winning cards. I can't seem to do much about it. I try to tell her to keep quiet, to stay discreet in the way she was throughout her life, but suddenly her voice is powerful.

"Granny, you've been dead for so long. Explain to me where you find the strength to shout so fiercely in my head?"

"*Maidele*, there's nothing to it. I haven't changed. My

voice is just what it used to be. It's just that your ears are unlocked now. And now you can hear . . . exactly in the way you heard me as a child and without the need for words, you understood everything. You remember those lullabies I sang for you? Remember? Everything was already in there . . ."

It's true my Granny didn't speak much, but she sometimes sang us lullabies in Yiddish. I didn't understand a word, but each time a melody rose up, it made the world around me tremble. And when she started to sing in my mind, I instantly recognized the song. It was easy: that was one everyone knew.

"Donna donna donna donna . . ." Granny sang.

"Granny, you mix everything up. That's not a Yiddish song, that's by Claude François. It's altogether French. The chorus goes, 'You'll miss the time . . . Donna donna donna . . . when you were a child.'"

"What? Who's this Claude François? He's a thief who steals songs from others and can't be bothered to write his own?"

"Granny, I assure you! *Donna Donna* is a classic French song."

"And since when exactly? No, my dear, not at all: it's a Yiddish song. He just stole it from us, that's all. Do you know what that song is about in Yiddish? No. Well, listen."

"Granny, I don't understand Yiddish."

"Just listen!"

So she started to sing:

"*Oyfn furl ligt a kelb*
Ligt gebundn mit a shtrik
Hoykh in himl flit a shvelbl
Freyt zikh dreyt zikh hin un krik . . ."

"On a wagon bound for market
there's a calf with a mournful eye.
High above him there's a swallow,
winging swiftly through the sky."[3]

[3] This translation comes from the English version of *Donna Donna*, sung by Joan Baez. It is a more literal translation of the original Yiddish version, by Scholem Sekunda and Aaron Zeitlin. The lyrics to the French version by Claude François can be translated as:

"Once upon a time there was a little boy
Who lived in a big house
His life was nothing but joy and happiness
And yet deep in his heart
He wanted to become big
Dreamed of being a man
Every night he thought about it
When his mother rocked him

"Donna, Donna, Donna, Donna
You'll miss the time
Donna, Donna, Donna, Donna
When you were a child

"Then he grew up, then he left
And he discovered life
Disappointed loves, hunger and fear
And often deep in his heart
He saw his childhood again

*

"Granny, stop. That's grotesque. I think I prefer Claude François' lyrics: the story of a little boy who knows that one day when he's old, he'll remember the joys of childhood with great nostalgia, with no mention of calves and markets."

"But it's rubbish, *Maidele*!"

"No, Granny, it's beautiful. It's talking about the happiness and tenderness of childhood."

"*Oy vey*! What happiness? What tenderness. You really want me to tell you about my childhood?"

"Of course, exactly. I'd like that a lot."

"No way. I'll never do it. I didn't do it while I was alive. So why would I, now that I'm dead. I prefer keeping *shtumm* about my history, I mean your history. And what would it change? You don't need to know that to know where you came from or to know the truth. And the truth is that your Claude François asked nothing of anyone, but just changed the lyrics of the song in order to pretend that life was sweet and full of nostalgia."

"Okay, Granny, but your Yiddish song doesn't say anything much deeper than that. It tells the story of a

"Dreamed of times gone by
Sadly he thought about it
And he remembered

"[chorus]

"Sometimes I think about that little boy
That little boy that I was."

little calf in his cart. It's sweet and bucolic. But it doesn't take us anywhere. In any case, where is this calf going in his cart? It doesn't tell us."

"Oh *Maidele* . . . Don't tell me you don't know where this little calf is going. Where do all the little calves of History go when they're in a cart?"

Silence. I keep quiet because I know too well. Little calves in all epochs—just like little Jewish children in some of them—always go to the same place: to *Pitchipoi*,[4] that last stop for all carts.

"*Oy a broch*, my little one . . . You see, you know. You too know this story. So listen to what it really says. Not the goy version by Claude François, but the real one.

"*Shrayt dos kelbl zogt der poyer*
Ver zhe heyst dikh zayn a kalb?
Volsts gekert tzu zayn a foygl
Volsts gekert zayn a shvalb."

"When the little calf weeps, the peasant says,
Whoever asked you to be a calf!
You would have been better off as a bird,
A little swallow that can fly away."

[4] *Pitchipoi* is the nonsense name used by Polish Jews for a Jewish ghetto. In the French wartime internment camp at Drancy, it was the name the displaced Jewish inmates gave to their imaginary destination—aka Auschwitz.

"But Granny, that's a horrible song. It's really cruel."

"*Oy vay*! And what do you think life is. Well, what do you think??"

I can see that she's getting agitated. I didn't want to exasperate her . . . only to take her in my arms.

"Tell me, Granny. Why don't the peasants ever stop the cart. Do you really think there's no one in history to save the little calves? Never?"

"Of course there is, *Maidele.* Listen, the song says it. There's someone to save the little calf. Donna, donna, donna."

"What? But who is that? Where does she come from?"

"Who? *Oy vay.* We don't know. Don't know if he exists. We don't even know if he can answer our call or if he hears our prayers. If he does, he doesn't answer because he doesn't speak Yiddish, the *schmuck.*"

Granny laughs, but I insist:

"But is donna, donna, donna Yiddish."

"No, it's not, it's a false name, a fake lead . . . like a coded message used to speak of someone else. Do you understand who, *Maidele*?"

"God? You're talking about God, right Granny?"

"No, no, it's the goys who call him that, those who believe in him . . . We Yids, we Jews, we always give him another name. Sometimes we call him ADONAI, but when we get a little intimate and it's been a very long time that we've been talking to him and he still doesn't give a damn, we give him sweet little nicknames."

And Granny started to sing again: "Adonai, Adonai,

Adonai, don . . . Do you understand now, my little one? The song in Yiddish, before Claude François made it into a peace-and-love pop number, says that no one is going to come and save the little calf. It says that neither the peasant, nor the swallow will ever do anything for the poor beast. No one will stop the slaughter that is luring his cart to *Pitchipoi*. It's true, God could save the calf. Obviously, he could stop it all. But if God was intervening in History, *Maidele*, we'd know it, wouldn't we?"

Granny carries on singing in Yiddish and I concentrate very hard on not crying. Because I need to keep the lock tightly closed to prevent my tears from overflowing.

I need to do everything to shore up the dikes of the world so that a sea of sorrow doesn't engulf us.

4
Conversation with Claude François

"My big little girl."

"Yes, Gramps."

"Do you know the grammatical rule that states—"

"Stop Gramps: I love you too and I miss you very much. You and I are so close even without grammar, I promise you. We don't need grammar to say those things you were never keen on saying to me while you were alive."

"No, no, your past participle use isn't quite right. It has to agree with the direct object when it's in front of the verb . . . you remember?"

"Yes, yes, I remember. Okay I can see you really want to talk about this, so I'm listening. Talk to me about correct grammar. Maybe it will help me think about something else. Since October 7, I can't think of anything at all, except that."

"I know. So listen to this. In fact, it's a rule for Hebrew."

"Hebrew? You, you're going to give me a Hebrew lesson?"

"Yes, but this particular grammatical rule, while specific to Hebrew, is almost universal. It could pertain to all languages. Listen, my big little girl: in biblical Hebrew, there's a grammatical form that concerns only verbs. The rule is called *VAV HA-IPOUKH.* In French it translates as the 'crochet renversant' the 'reversible hook.'"

"It sounds like a Karate hold or Kung Fu sequence. An ippon."

"Yes, you're right. In fact, it's a little like that, and you'll see, it really is something to fall over backwards for. But listen to this: the Hebrew conjugation is quite simple."

And that's how my grandfather reappeared from the big beyond where he had retired over thirty years ago to take up his grammarian's service again. He re-joined the "citizen reserve force" of my conscience to give me a lesson in conjugation.

"You should know that in Hebrew, every verb can be conjugated in the present, the past or the future. There are no imperfects or narrative pasts or past tenses using auxiliary verbs. In Hebrew there is only a single tense for talking about what is past. It's called the past accomplished. I ate, I drank, I walked . . . there, it's done. It's over. It's behind me. You see me, for example: I lived and I died. Hahaha."

"Go on, Gramps."

"The future is a verb conjugated in the unfinished: I will be. I will see. I will say, etc. But in Hebrew this is complicated by an odd grammatical tool. A very small word, in fact a single letter of the alphabet, holds considerable, indeed overwhelming power."

"You don't think you're overdoing things a little with your 'considerable' and 'overwhelming.'"

"Just hold on: this letter is called the *vav* and in Hebrew it's pronounced as a simple 'v' and looks like a stick or staff—straight like an 'I' it can also be drawn as a 'hook.' It looks like a little nail when you look at it close up. And just imagine, placed next to any noun, it translates as an 'and.' You know, the conjunction that combines—"

"Gramps, pleeease. Let's not go over the whole primary school syllabus. I'm not a little girl anymore."

"Well, if you say so . . . The letter *vav* designates the link, the relation, the little nail that links things together. Do you follow me? So imagine that if you nail it to a verb and not to a noun, it no longer has the same function at all. Attached to a verb, it suddenly no longer links one word to another, but acquires a magic power. It becomes the master of time."

"What? What on earth are you on about?"

"Demonstration: if in Hebrew I write, 'I spoke' and if I draw this little *vav* in front of the verb, *abracadabra*, my phrase suddenly means 'I will speak.' Same thing the other way round: if I write a phrase in the future, like 'I will say' and I add my magic letter just in front, I transform 'I will speak' into 'I spoke.' Truly."

"But that's crazy."

"Completely. And it's great, right? With a little nothing letter, Hebrew reverses time. A little nail planted just there transforms the past into the future, and the future into the past. Do you see why we call this rule the 'reversing hook?' All by itself it reverses the tense of a sentence. Don't try and tell me grammar isn't the most extraordinary thing in the world."

"*Maidele*, you called me?"

"No Granny, I was talking to Gramps. He explained some extraordinary grammar to me."

"Ah, okay. I heard 'extraordinary granma,' so I thought that—"

"Did you know the rule about the 'reversible hook' in Hebrew, which turns the past into the future and the future into the past?"

"Of course I know it! And so? What's so special?"

"Well, it's really surprising to find . . ."

"Really? You think . . . ? Why? It's always like that in life, isn't it?"

"What?"

"Well that hook, it always makes the link between the past and the future. Whatever happened will always happen again. If it happened in the past, why wouldn't it be the same once more? You have to be a real shmuck to imagine that what happens after has nothing to do with what happened before. It's the same nail after all."

"Granny, I don't understand what you're talking about. This here is about grammar."

"Exactly. Hebrew grammar tells you there's a link, a hook between what we lived in the past and what happens today, that's all. You always end up repeating something in the belief that it wasn't said before. But the past never goes away. You know that . . . if not, your Gramps and I, we wouldn't be here, stuck in your head. You nailed us there. And it's not so that I could tell you about the past: you know very well that I won't say anything . . . It's so that we could tell you about what happens next. That's all. That's why you've been talking to us all the time over these past weeks. You see. Because things repeat themselves throughout time."

"Things repeat?"

"For sure, things repeat . . . *Maidele, Maidele* . . . You know what—it's exactly like that song you love. You know. The one that goy sings."

"Claude François?"

"Yes, him."

"Oh no, Granny. Don't start that again. And what on earth is the link with Claude François? We've already talked about his song, about God, the calves, and the slaughterhouse. That's enough."

"No, no, I'm not talking about that song. He sings another. Very well known. You remember . . . It says that it's happened, and it will happen again . . . Like in your grammar, you see. With just a little *vav, w*hoops, the past becomes the future. You understand, don't you, what he means in this song: he's talking about us, about Jews. Well, about those who detest us, the antisemites, who will blame us again and again . . . cause it never stops."

"But stop saying any old thing, Granny. You're delirious. Claude François never wrote anything like that."

"But he did! It's just that he's clever, that *mamzer* . . . well at least until he tried to change a bulb in his bath. But before that he was clever to sing that song and pretend he was talking about something else. But if you listen carefully, it's easy to understand what he's talking about."

"You say any old thing!"

"Okay, so you don't want to hear it. But you can see it clearly. He's surrounded by those dancing girls, the Claudettes, his clothes every color of the rainbow, singing his *Chanson populaire*, his 'popular song,' and that's when he says, bopping around all the while, 'It goes away and it returns, it's made up of little nothings.' It's clear he's talking about antisemitism. You think it's going away, but it always comes back. That song is about us, *Maidele*. What else could it be about?"

5
Conversation with Antiracists

"*And . . . it goes away and it returns . . . it's made up of little nothings . . . it can be sung and it can be danced. And it comes back. It stays in your mind like a pop refrain.*"

It's uncanny. Now that song is forever in my head.

It's crazy how it takes hold of you. It may be old, but it doesn't seem to date. It's really popular and at this moment even populist. It's a hit everywhere—number one in the top 50 hatreds that make the world dance.

These antisemites are strong. They appropriate so much, even the refrains of pop songs and advertising slogans. They're everywhere. And their marketing is good.

Just look at what they've managed to do with a simple word they invented.

In the 19th century, one of them, a certain Wilhelm Marr, said to himself: "What a shame that we don't have a term to describe our great humanist battle for a better world." And right away, he gives his political party the name "Anti-Semitic League," to excite the electorate. It was a *bric à brac* name concocted from a vague reference to Semites, a biblical grouping that evoked something barbaric and out-of-date. And Bingo, it worked. It met with enormous success: the brand developed and opened subbranches.

Of course, the concept existed well before him, indeed millennia before he launched his particular brand of hatred. But it didn't yet have so clear a tag: antisemitism—sophisticated and simple at the same time. Clearly the concept was attractive, and its clientele was motivated. The proof is that it still sells all over the place. Whether we realize it or not, the brand is foisted on all of us. It's a real monopoly.

A century and a half after Marr popularized it, we all use the term. We do so as if words didn't have a history. As if the words weren't freighted with the ideology of those who invented it. Madness. Perhaps the term should be boycotted or at least kept at a distance. We need to move away from the haters and the words they invent. But it isn't easy to do.

Maybe certain terms could be privileged over others. We could use "Judeophobia" in antisemitism's place. But that doesn't quite work either. Why would hatred of Jews be phobic? What fear would it be a name for? That remains mysterious. For some two thousand years, books have been written to try and illuminate the enigma—without success. The subject remains murky.

We don't have any better idea of what it means to "be Jewish" than of what it means to "detest Jews." We only know that Judaism is transmitted through the mother and antisemitism through bitterness, a terrible acrimony that nothing mollifies nor explains. Is it contagious? Can it be cured? Who knows?

What we do know, however, is that this hatred is not at all like others. Here's the proof: if you're racist, if you hate blacks, or Chinese, or redheads, or weightlifters, that's shameful and pitiable. But that hatred will give you no *a priori* explanation of the world. It won't help you understand its crises, its poisoning, or its creeping rot. It won't resolve any of your existential doubts. On the other hand, antisemitism has a far broader remit in its sales pitch and that's why it goes down so well:

"*Come closer ladies and gentlemen, come one, come all, come and see what I've got for you. On my stand you'll find not just a flimsy bit of trumpery, but a solid product that you can keep and with a little luck transmit in good shape to your children. This magic product, which you all need even if you don't know it, Ladies and Gentlemen, is called 'hatred of the Jew.' It comes with numerous accessories. If you choose hatred of the Jew, Ladies and Gentlemen, it comes with a wondrous explanatory schema for understanding the whole world. Hate the Jews and you'll have in hand a solution for all the ills of the planet, not to mention a super-effective stain remover to rid yourself of all personal responsibility while foisting it on another. Thanks to this altogether (or almost) free hatred, you'll instantly have access to expertise in the world economy, geopolitics, sometimes even in virology. You'll understand why the market collapses, why the bank of Rothschild pulls the strings of global lobbies, why the media confiscate truth and Covid spreads. Above all, you'll know whom crime benefits. You'll see through the global conspiracies propagated by this small, dispersed group who are in charge of the world's most sophisticated shenanigans. Ladies and Gentlemen, some toys come without batteries, but the hatred of Jews comes with a powerful battery of explanations of the world, one that's rechargeable in all circumstances, particularly in times of crisis. So don't hesitate, Ladies and Gentlemen. Come closer. It's Christmas soon."*

This scenario is hardly new. It's been lived by many generations in very different periods and places. The novelist Albert Cohen, for example, recounts in *Ô vous, frères humains (Oh You, Brother Humans)*, the day that as a child he came across his own hawker of hatred. He recognizes how much this encounter at the age of ten shaped him as a man and as the writer he became. He remembers the hawker's words, addressed to a laughing crowd exulting at the humiliation of the Jewish child. Again and again in his mind and in ours, the hawker repeats, "Dirty Jew . . . He rolls in gold and smokes fat cigars while we tighten our belts, isn't that so, Ladies and Gentlemen? You . . . you can get out of here now. We've seen enough of you. You aren't at home here. This isn't your country [. . .] Go on, run, get out of here and visit Jerusalem for a bit."

The purveyors of anti-Jewish hatred sing all the same tunes today. They frequent the same markets, occupy the same stalls and harangue the laughing crowds with the very same products. Almost word for word, their monologues are the same. Almost . . . but not quite. Back then, in the time of Albert Cohen or even of Wilhelm Marr, Jews were told to go and "seek out Jerusalem," "run off to Palestine" to free Europe of their presence. Now, the opposite is shouted. "Leave Jerusalem"; "Free Palestine" of your presence, your history or, better still, your life.

Another difference: back then the hate merchant was simultaneously flogging both some antisemitic tat and some racist baubles. His hatred stall was very well stocked: you could imagine he had enough for everyone. These days, paradoxically, it's often in the name of antiracism that he fires off his harangue. The wares on his stand include the defence of the widow and the ragged orphan, concern about the poor and the disadvantaged. This acute awareness of the fate of the unfortunate authorizes him to hate legally and while keeping his dignity intact. So, he can spit in the face of a Jewish child, or rip his photo down from a wall if someone has had the gall to remind the world that he was kidnapped.

"But that's got nothing to do with it," the good souls shout. "This is simply anti-Zionism. We've got nothing against Jewish children, only Israeli ones." So that's okay then, is it? They are all ineluctably guilty?

This has already been said, but perhaps to repeat it

is now necessary especially as History itself now seems to stutter. Both racism and antisemitism need and will always need to be opposed with the same vigour. To tolerate one in the name of the other is disgraceful. Nonetheless, to combat them it's important to recognize that they don't grow out of exactly the same mental structure.

Take the racist, for example: he usually says, "I am more, or better, than you. Because you don't belong to the right nationality or the right culture. Your civilisation is not at the level of mine." The antisemite's expresses something a little different. In the form of a question, he asks the Jew: "Why are you where I ought to be? Why do you have what I should have had—access to power, to money, to land, to good luck?"

The antisemite, like Calimero, the black cartoon chick in a family of yellow chickens, repeats to all and sundry, "It's just too unfair!" The antisemite, though, is far less likeable than Calimero. Full of hate, he sees himself as the victim of terrible inequality. He is deprived of something, it has been taken from him, usurped. He has been cheated by life or by a neighbour, by his wife's lover, by his banker or by God, it doesn't matter which. But he knows very well where all this started. Where the racist has a superiority complex, the antisemite sees himself diminished, amputated.

So it is that these two detestable hatreds, the racist's and the antisemite's don't emerge from the same mental space. Nothing, of course, prevents the two from coming together. Some people immerse themselves in both kinds of dirt: they combine marvellously.

I remember a time that those under thirty won't. For many of us back then, it was clear that the battle against racism and antisemitism was one. We knew we couldn't overcome one without mobilizing against the other. I continue to believe that, and I refuse to establish a hierarchy of hates. But I feel much more alone today. There are many people around us who are convinced that to mobilise on the side of one entails a lack of empathy for the others. It's absurd that one must struggle to counter these convictions.

Many of my "friends"—and I put scare quotes around the word until clarification comes—said to me a few weeks ago: "There no question of our going to the demonstration against antisemitism, because in that crowd there'll be uninhibited racists."[5] I confess to being silenced by their argument. They preferred leaving the Jews on their own at a demonstration targeting the hatred of Jews. They chose not to join those whom they claim they defend, only to avoid running across those they disdain in the crowd. I ask myself whether they'll decide not to go to the wedding or funeral of their best friend, because they fear meeting a batty great uncle

[5] On 12th November all the French political parties, including the far right Front National, but excluding the left now called France Unbowed, demonstrated against antisemitism in the face of a "steep rise in antisemitic actions since October 7"—Hugh Schofield, BBC News Paris. November 12 2023

there who is a racist or a misogynist. I don't really know. As it happens, they clearly signposted their priorities.

Do they think it gave me pleasure to march with the heirs of the National Front? I would have preferred it if my "friends" had decided to rally with me in the antiracist struggle I have always been involved with, so that together we could turn the party of the extreme right into a mere "historical" detail. Apparently, that's no longer possible.

These days hatred against the Jews is paradoxically fuelled by so-called antiracism. A brilliant shorthand is at work: let's be on the side of the weak, the victims, the vulnerable. The problem is that while the list of victims is long and vast, the Jews don't appear in it. Strange. Even when they're assassinated, defenestrated, burned, tortured, raped, or kidnapped: nothing renders them vulnerable enough to be worthy of protection. Their vulnerability always remains something to be demonstrated.

It's almost as if, even when they're wounded or dead, they remain rich and powerful. Maybe that's why Jewish graves and funeral stones are attacked, sometimes the very corpses themselves. There's a supposition that somehow even in death they stay strong and in control. Maybe they even run the media and the financial world from the Beyond—who knows?

I rather like this idea: the Muslims promise seventy virgins in paradise. Why not have the Jews promise seventy television channels and leads for the Dow Jones?

Yes, let's laugh. But none of this rhetoric is actually new. It just has unexpected variants these days. As the song says: "It goes away and it comes back . . . it's made up of little nothings."

Sometimes these little nothings are insults or simply implications. Most of the time, they are eruptions of petty cowardice. There are those who hear and recognize the old forms of hate speech, and some who are deaf to them, unwittingly or not. They say they hear only silence, or a vague rumble, like tinnitus, which doesn't mean anything much to them. No, no, they affirm, it isn't antisemitism: "Stop seeing that everywhere. You're the ones who end up creating it."

Take this example: When one of our former prime ministers talks of "the financial domination of the media, the world of the arts and music," who is he talking about? I don't know. When the Antivaxxers point a finger at a pharmaceutical lobby responsible for the health crisis, who are they denouncing? I have no idea. When some of the *Gilets Jaunes* condemn the stranglehold of the powerful which usurps the power of the people, who are they referring to? The cat's stolen my tongue.

How am I to know? The word Jew had never been uttered. The language is vague and the accusation shrouded.

And *voilà* the old gang of far-rightists are back, those of the antisemitic *Rivarol* magazine and the Soral sect, and they salute old P.M. Dominique de Villepin as a great statesman. The old anti-Jewish slogans suddenly unfurl during the Antivax protests, and the Rothschild bank is named time and again during the gatherings of the *Gilets Jaunes.*

And what is the economist Jacques Attali, born to a Jewish family in Algeria, doing in a piece of street graffiti in Avignon that shows him holding the strings of a Pinocchio-like puppet wearing Emmanuel Macron's face? How exactly should I be reading that?

Are they trying to tell us something? Well, not necessarily! Unless . . .

It's right at the tip of my tongue . . . but no, no, it escapes me!

"Stop seeing antisemitism everywhere!" they tell me indignantly. "Yes, yes, I promise. I'll stop."

"We're telling you these people aren't antisemitic!" Yes, absolutely. I'm altogether prepared to believe it. You're right, they aren't. No, they aren't. But isn't it mysterious that they speak that language? Antisemitism and its long-inherited phraseology leaps onto their lips and speaks through them. It's a breathtaking act of ventriloquism. It diffuses an imperceptible sort of ultrasound, just strong enough so that somehow the antisemitic pack receives it.

They're happy just to move their lips, nothing more: the word "Jew" is never uttered. And yet, abracadabra, they manage to unleash a bizarre essence from a distance, a sound that comes not from their mouths, but from their guts . . . And all of a sudden, the intestines of society erupt in flatulence, as if they knew how to open sphincters remotely. They speak here, and the excrement is dropped elsewhere.

It's worthy of a great magical spectacle. The mouth that mutters something and the stomach that absorbs something different. Sometimes we're even told that it's altogether against the will of the speaker. Fascinating. It's even ravishing in a literal sense. It ravishes attention and intelligence; it bewitches subjugated consciences. Oh yes, "It is sung, it is danced, it's remembered over and again, like the refrain of a popular song!"

6
Conversation with Rose

Rose will die soon. She writes to me about it and her children tell me. It's imminent and everyone seems to know it. She feels herself to be at the end of the road. It's the image she always uses to begin our conversation, to propose that we talk together about it.

Talk is not quite the right word. Rose doesn't speak. She hasn't done so for a long time. She suffers from an illness, the name of which makes you shiver as soon as you hear it—amyotrophic lateral sclerosis, though most think of it more simply as Charcot's disease or Lou Gehrig's disease. One by one muscles stop functioning and paralysis sets in, first the limbs and then the respiratory system. Nervous degeneration spreads rapidly and leads to death. Well before that the illness affects speech and elocution. Rose stopped talking long before I met her. She manages a few sounds, but it's a machine that does her talking for her. She writes and technology speaks in her place.

In the own way, Rose became a ventriloquist: her lips hardly move and one of her fingers touches the screen, then her voice emerges from a processor balanced on her stomach. Speech is no longer there, but the conversation is so powerful, it grabs you by the gut.

A few months ago, her children sent me an email because she wanted to meet me and ask me to accompany her on her difficult last journey. I needed to attempt to walk down her path, since she no longer could, and to find the words she could no longer speak.

From our very first encounter when the door of her apartment opened, I understood that the road we would travel would be more luminous than I had imagined when I had responded to the appeal. Like the sunbeam that came through her bay window and illuminated her living room, all around her something shone. There were trinkets, books, and a great deal of love. And amid objects of the kind that can often recount a life far better than words, she waited for me, straight backed and determined, with a will to keep the conversation going despite her handicap.

She handed me a piece of paper on which she had written a few words. "There are a thousand things I'd like to talk about with you." Her face had a particular glow.

She tapped letters, one after another, onto the screen and did so with the single digit over which she still had a modicum of control. She then pressed a green button at the bottom of her text and that's when the voice that speaks for her, spoke.

Technology changes everything in the life of the ill. It permits an escape from complete imprisonment inside a body.

Rose's synthetic voice resonates and I jump: the tone and expression is exactly that of the GPS in the car that brought me to her: "In 100 metres turn left . . . At the first roundabout, take the second exit . . ." The intonation is the same, as is the slightly choppy flow, except that what is being indicated is an altogether different map.

The evident gap between the written message and its digital voicing has a comic side effect, as unexpected as it is misplaced. I have to bite my cheek to make sure my smile is under control. It's not so easy. The same monotonous voice that guides my movements in the city and stops me getting lost is playing against type. It's like a casting error. Used to giving out banal road directions, the voice is now engaged in setting out a different kind of directive. The profane tone is speaking a sacred language:

"I'm afraid of dying," it says as if announcing "A speed camera on your right in twenty yards." "I'm frightened for my children," replaces "Turn around as soon as possible."

Is existence compatible with the language of GPS? Is the distance to be covered still long? Will the traffic still move? And what if at the next roundabout, there's no exit?

Rose is quickly sensitive to the face I make. She guesses my discomfort and drawing a smile writes, "I have a lovely voice, don't I? I could work for the railways." The remark sets the tone for our conversation. We have both decided that on this bumpy road towards a death already announced, we'll only take short cuts in which absurd humor reigns and fear is a dead end.

And so, we established a ritual for our conversation.

We started to write to one another every week. Every Friday either one or the other of us took the initiative.

At first the roles were clear. We each knew our part. I asked for her news and interrogated her about her week. I worried over her body and her thoughts. In brief, I was the rabbi, and she the sick one. It was simple. I did what I had had to do many times before: accompany the dead while trying to maintain the distance apposite to my function, which, to those who call on it, speaks through me of a tradition far greater than me alone. Its wisdom precedes me and will outlive me, and if it speaks to you through my body, in that moment it's because it's speaking through me, as it speaks to you. In fact, I too, in the exercise of my profession, am often something of a ventriloquist . . . In the language of the Jewish tradition, I would say that I'm "*dybbukhed*," inhabited by a heritage that speaks through me. It traverses generations, travels when needed through my lips. It has and will continue to be spoken by many others. It is a better guide than GPS and has had 3000 years of practice saying to the Jews "Your destination will be reached . . . or not. Beware: there have been quite a few accidents on the route."

Rose often talks to me of her worries, but also very precisely of her hopes. Not of getting better or surviving, but of reaching dates she has randomly set for herself, a little like highway tollgates you've promised yourself you'd reach before stopping for the night.

She is determined to hold her yet unborn granddaughter in her arms, then to get through the autumn and to see its amazing beauty from her window, or to reach the birthday of a loved one and then, oh why not, to celebrate the end of the year holidays . . .

We talk of the way in which time, as death approaches, unfolds so strangely, a day suddenly able to last an entire season or a week a billion years. We tell ourselves time and again that everything dies—hopes, ideas, loves, illusions. And our awareness of their finiteness makes us a little more alive.

We talk a lot about her family, her passions, her past loves and above all of her children whom she holds dear above all, of her parents too, and of her Jewish heritage. For a long time, she felt herself a foreigner to this history, but suddenly, it signalled to her and she wasn't insensitive to its call.

We talked about the man she loved, of their powerful bond and the particular attentiveness he brought to her in her illness. One day, during our intimate conversation, he burst into the room and inadvertently cut off my words. She hurriedly tapped out on the screen a devastating comment that stopped him in his tracks. And the GPS voice blurted out in a sassy tone: "Leave us alone!" All three of us all but died laughing, which meant of course we were very much alive.

Then, October 7 happened. "Happened to us," I should say. Death shook us violently, but not in the way we had anticipated. Instead, Jewish history paid us a visit with its own kind of bereavements and hauntings. It brought with it the feeling that we now had to face the reverberations of the past head on. Suddenly it was no longer a question of Rose's death, but of that of a world. Our conversation shifted abruptly. It's hard for me even now to clearly explain what transpired. Perhaps it's too early. What I know is that very quickly, a memory came back to me: it involved accompanying another person towards their death. After October 7, while tending to Rose, I was suddenly filled with the echo of another grief, one that seemed to bear no connection at all. This is how death works: when it strikes, it always brings its prior visits with it. It reminds us of the whole history of its comings and goings in our lives.

Several years back I had accompanied a man of my own age towards death. A very different kind of illness took him away. It had spared his voice, but it destroyed his body. We both knew that his end was imminent. His family knew it too. All his near ones, his wife, his children, and his friends were close to me, and I loved them dearly. They were part of my circle of intimate friends, and his death shook me terribly. A witness to their suffering, faced by the despair of those dear to me, unlike them, I nonetheless had a role to fill. So, I engaged in a process I knew well. I anesthetized my own suffering as best as I could in order to carry out my function. I made certain to find the right distance, the one that permits you to be at the side of those who walk the indescribable path of bereavement. I held up. I stayed solid for the length of the journey, even when Marc said goodbye to his children, even at the last tollgate he had marked out for himself, even on the day of his last breath, and even while preparing his funeral service. I held out during the lifting of the body and throughout the ceremony I had carefully prepared. Not once did my voice flinch, nor my eyes weep at the sight of the stricken faces of his near ones. I saw that they clung to my words and to the rite that I carried as to an unsinkable raft: someone had to pretend to stay the course.

It was at the end of the ceremony while they were all hugging each other that a stranger in the crowd came up to me. He murmured a few words in my ear, a perfectly anodyne phrase, but one for which I hadn't prepared myself.

"I imagine all this can't have been easy for you."

The words echoed through my head and at that moment, a man whom I had never seen before and would not see again, a perfect stranger who had no idea what he had unleashed in me, shattered all my defences.

"I imagine it can't have been easy for you."

That single phrase destroyed my suit of armour and dismantled my mental defenses. I had no choice but to look beneath the chain mail and see the oozing wound and all the misery I had stashed there. I recalled that my friend was dead: my rabbinical function could no longer eclipse my misery. Down with the masks. On that central path of a large Paris cemetery, I was overcome by a heaving sob and carried away by an unspeakable pain. My total destitution lay uncovered, the bottomless vulnerability of a being who at the burial of a near one can do nothing but cry. There was absolutely nothing else to do.

After October 7, in my weekly conversations with Rose and through all the e-mails we exchanged, a similar thing happened without my being aware of it. Rose unmasked me. At the threshold of her own death, and while death was all around us—in doctors' diagnoses, in the faces of young people assassinated for having gone dancing, in the images of the growing piles of children's corpses—a conversation began for which I hadn't prepared myself.

Rose handed me a mirror which forced me to see my own face and not just hers. Her own words, written or uttered by the machine, somehow managed forcibly to turn my "how are you?" back on myself. Not as a polite question returned to a visitor who sits by your bedside to pose it. No. Suddenly in each of our exchanges she had managed a unique way of turning towards me when I thought I was turning towards her. Her way of listening placed me without my being prepared for it in the strange position of an alter ego.

A vulnerable human facing a vulnerable human. "A woman whom death visits" in conversation with "a woman whom death visits." Two bereaved beings who know that nothing will ever be again as it was before. Her paralysis echoed mine, just as her solitude did. And I knew that I would never fully find my voice again.

She started asking me for my news. In my silences and my sighs, she would read my real answers, those I didn't ever utter. It was as if, better than anyone else, she knew my despair, the morbid terror that had sprung up in my soul and which wasn't foreign to it.

Traditionally, we always read psalms to the ill. It's an ancestral poetry intended to calm them and keep them company. Amongst all these poems, repeated in so many circumstances that one ends up no longer hearing them, there is one in particular, that is always sung at the bedside of the suffering. We imbue its words with an almost magic power. "Though I walk through the valley of the shadow of death, I fear no harm, for You are with me." (Psalm 23)

The "You" in this verse who walks by our side through the valleys of despair is none other than the divine, whom we imagine accompanies us in the terrifying night of our solitude. These last weeks, by Rose's side, it seemed to me we were continually murmuring these words for each other. Because in the valley of the shadow of death which surrounded us, neither of us was unscathed, nor was either of us alone.

Perhaps I became for her another rabbi or "not just" a rabbi: not only someone who, with the emotional distance of her function, communicates the immutable and solid matter of tradition. But someone who admits how devastated and inconsolable she is. Someone who, ever on the brink of tears, knows that the field of ruins in front of her is in her own image. I shared with Rose my woman's pain—my pain as mother, as a Jew, as a "Jewish mother," and I confided my pastoral difficulties to her, my writing projects—something I would never have done before in my pastoral role. It seems to me now that perhaps Rose and October 7 turned me into a different woman, certainly into a different rabbi.

Rose is going to die. I know that. But I still don't know how to say thank you to her. I have only a few days or perhaps a few weeks left, but I would like to have the time to find the correct words. That, too, is why I am writing. To tell her, if it isn't too late, that she allows me to stay upright while the ground beneath our feet has given way. Since October 7, her way of listening, her hearing without words, has changed my way of listening forever. At the gates of death, she has given me a life lesson that has made me hear something completely new with perfect eloquence. She has changed my path.

"Recalculating your new route now . . ."

7
Conversation with My Children

"Have you nothing better to do?"

Is each generation condemned to repeat the exact same phrases? Apparently, the answer is yes. Those words heard so often in childhood, are the ones I now speak to my children in order to establish the same authority. Or almost the same. I need to tell them that there are things to learn and know in life that go beyond simple entertainment.

"Pick up a book, why don't you!"

I've become that oldie who uses the same stock phrases that were directed to her by other oldies—whom, of course, she told off for doing so. It's crazy how time brings us close to our parents. Our children take their revenge by transforming us into our parents. It's the relentless chain of the generations.

I was told to turn off the television, and now I threaten to cut off the wi-fi. Apart from the technology itself, there's no real difference. The generational conflict is almost the same. It deviates a bit, then it is resolved just as it always has been: a few shaky compromises so that you feel you haven't quite given in.

"You can keep watching only if you change to something a little less idiotic than what you've got on there now!" "Get rid of Tik Tok and Snapchat. Watch a documentary or a history series."

In my childhood, we negotiated in almost the same way. It involved exchanging stupidity for pedagogy. I remember a single television series we were never prevented from watching. It was meant to make us more cultured, so why put a prohibition on it? Its educational gloss somehow made it "*kosher*," fit to be consumed at any time of day. It was thus the supreme argument for lengthening the screen time allowed to us.

I'm sure all French children of my generation remember this program—the harpsichord melody that accompanied the opening credits is unforgettable: "Tatata . . . tatatatataaa . . . taaaaaaa . . ."

Bach's Fugue in D minor rang out our temporary salvation and gifted us a 26-minute pass. A monkey appeared on screen. He got up on two legs, became a Neanderthal, then a hunter-gatherer, before donning a Greek toga, converting himself into a Renaissance painter, jumping on the barricades of the French Revolution only to land in a sports car before finally taking off in a rocket. The message was clear: all of human history could be expressed in one toccata.

The "Once Upon a Time . . . Humans" series, which screened for decades, contained a very seductive message: the wheels of History turn.

The presenter was always a man called Pierre, who

had a sympathetic face. He showed up in all periods, whether prehistoric or in 1968. His son was called Pierrot and his daughter Pierrette. They had uproarious adventures, inflected by the period they were in. It must have been exhausting, all the more so because they always met the same sinister character who put spokes in their wheels even before the wheel had been invented.

In a corner of the screen, the date of the goings-on changed. A little rectangle indicated the period: Renaissance, Monarchy, First World War . . . The costumes, too, changed, but the drama was continuous. I would often ask myself how you got from one timeframe to another, and more generally who was this man in History who one day awoke, calmy opened his shutters, turned toward his wife, and said: "My dear, that's it. Antiquity is over! We're in the Middle Ages. Put on your best tonight, I'm taking you out to light a pyre." Who knows how the past passes and the future takes over? No one.

If I liked this series, it's because it told us, complete with parental benediction, that it's simple to narrate History, and that in the flow of generations, there is stability. Everything changes, but nothing changed. The world evolves, but something eternal persists—solid, like a Pierre (whose name means stone).

I don't know what influence this series had on my generation. It should have convinced us that humanity doesn't change and that according to that logic, the sinister characters regularly come back. We should have learned that the sentence for Pierre and his children would never come to an end. But we wanted to believe something else. So instead, we told ourselves that a new era had begun with us. And after all that humanity had been through, it now understood and was moving into a new phase.

October 7 made that damned toccata resonate through my mind again. A concerto in G which collapses. I watched my children without saying anything. I was too afraid of the words that might come out of me. I certainly didn't want to hear myself repeat what was screaming so noisily in my mind.

I left them to their screens, hoping that the algorithm would keep the images of the world's violence at a distance. It was idiotic on my part.

Very quickly they saw exactly what I wished they wouldn't see. And the questions came. My children, each in their own way and with words that befitted their age, asked me to explain the same thing: Tell us mother, why is it happening again? And why always and again is the first stone hurled at us Jews?

I dreamed that I could explain this to them in a television series, somehow adapt what I had seen in my childhood into a more credible version. Something that was easy to narrate. It would be called, "Once upon a time . . . (there was?) antisemitism."

Over the credits, rather than Bach, I would opt for Wagner, a bona fide classic. I would choose *Ride of the Valkyries,* or better still *The Flying Dutchman* . . . because that's what it's all about, those historical phantoms that always return.

True, I would have had to invent a main character. I wouldn't have called him Pierre. I would have found him a more Jewish name, perhaps even a Yiddish surname. Why not Schlemiel? In Yiddish, that name is always given to the fool or the unlucky one in any group. A *Schlemiel* is the one whose bread always falls on the buttered side, the man who decides to open an umbrella shop at the very moment that drought sets in. Many tales and legends attempt to illuminate the origin of this mythical character. One I particularly like is that at the beginning a great Talmudic sage bore the name. One day he went off to study far from home. And he discovered, with great emotion, that in his absence his faithful wife had given birth to a son . . . eleven months after his departure.[6] Ever since then Schlemiel is the name given to all the unlucky ones in history, the cheated, the cuckolded, the awkward and clumsy. If there's lightning, it always strikes *them*. "Once upon a time . . . Jewish bad luck."

The pitch for this TV series is simple: the lead is always the same and his clothes vary only slightly with the change of period: a distinguishing yellow circle, a pointed hat, a yellow star . . . nothing actually changes all that much. Cruelly, antisemitic fashions lack imagination. Just look at the drawings, etchings, or period paintings: the Jew always has more or less the same

[6] From the Talmudic scholar known as Maharil or Rabbi Yaakov ben Moshe Levi Moelin (1360-1427) who codified the customs of the German Jews.

physiognomy: a big, hooked nose, ears sticking out, witchy hair. The other essential details are invariably his large hands with their grasping fingers. "All the better to manipulate you with, my child!" Because fundamentally that's what the Jew is always accused of: manipulating the world. That's why in so many images in the museum of antisemitic horrors, he holds the terrestrial globe in his hands, or pulls the strings of another actor, usually a banker, a politician, or a freemason. The Jew is the great puppet-master of the world, the famous conjuror. Nothing disappears into his hat, of course, since he's the one forced to wear it.

And with what talent he's portrayed! Just look at the cunning trick: he's capable of being guilty at the very same time of one thing and its opposite. Depending on the episode, Schlemiel is accused of being too rich and too poor, of producing excessively or inversely of living off society as a parasite. At one and the same time he can be a "capitalist bastard" or "a Bolshevik rat." He exasperates if he's too discreet and not easily identifiable. At the same time, he's reproached for his "bling" or for showing off. What arrogance he displays! He's everywhere. He disturbs because he wanders and doesn't settle. But he's even more detestable when he claims sovereignty and demands a land. And do you know what on top of that? It seems he even invented patriarchy. It's in his texts and literary heritage. But it's also said that he's at the origin of feminist revolt, the very one that threatens the natural order of things and proper family values.

Oh my, oh my he's so powerful to be able to be both this and that at the same time. You can understand how this threatens the antisemites who have invented him in this way, and who throughout history try to eradicate him. How could it be otherwise? How could these good people forgive him for what he has forced them to do? Why should they excuse him for stimulating such hatred?

"Once upon a time . . . the antisemite!"

In the series there would be an infinite number of seasons. Because this hatred stretches across history and geography. It's everywhere and indestructible. It only changes its name and face according to the episode. Some would like to believe that the producer is always of the right . . . because in the last century, that's who held the greatest number of episodes in the series.

Others say on the contrary, it's the extreme left that today is responsible for the greatest transmission and manages even the publicity.

Unless hatred of the Jews always remains a co-production: neither of the right or the left, but rather potentially of both. The market is much too significant for a single actor to monopolise it. That's what the anti-trust laws preventing monopoly mean.

Be that as it may, the timeless power of antisemitism in fact seems to lie in its object's capacity for change. The Jew is endowed with a fundamental plasticity: it permits him to be adapt better than anyone else to what each period of history asks of him.

Tatata . . . tatatataaa . . . taaaaaaa . . .

Each new context manufactures images and language. These are in constant evolution. Thus Schlemiel will be "guilty" in each epoch of being what that society most fears.

In the Middle Ages, what is most feared are contagious illnesses, the plague and cholera. People are obsessed by the purification of the body or of ideas. Never mind: just make the Jew a contaminating agent, accuse him of perverting water sources or texts, of poisoning wells or ideas.

During our contemporary pandemic, the Covid conspiracy theorists simply resuscitated the old antisemitic plots. They turned the Jews into leaders of pharmaceutical lobbies who spread the virus. Well yes, why not recycle what had worked so well in the past!

In the fascist society of the 1930's, the model of male virility wins the support of the masses. They look for leaders with a powerful masculinity and a testosterone-fuelled speech. The market adapts itself: the Jew is almost instantly transformed into a feminized wimp, an intellectual with no virility. Léon Blum, the French Jewish and Socialist prime minister, is then criticized for his high-pitched voice and his soft politics. The antisemitic caricatures pick up a misogynistic streak: Jews love money, contact with the strong, they're untrustworthy, lascivious, hysterical . . . in short, just like women. They're often drawn with a bosom and swaying hips.

Nothing new under the sun: in the Middle Ages numerous pamphlets affirmed that Jewish men had monthly periods. It was said that they bled monthly from the scar of their absent foreskin, or by rectal haemorrhage.

Almost nothing changes . . .

Almost . . . because we are now suddenly propelled into a different historical moment.

Since #MeToo and the legitimate battle for the rights of women and sexual minorities, it seems Jews themselves have "transitioned." Abracadabra, the Jew who used to be gendered female, has now acquired all the exclusive traits of the alpha male. The Jew now incarnates an image of indomitable masculinity. A new hate figure has entered our sights: the Israeli soldier, square jawed and displaying powerful muscles. In this new symbolic role, the Jew becomes a male who engenders evil.

This makes things very complicated for militant feminists who want to denounce the massacres of October 7. What if the women who were raped and killed are a little too soldierly and masculine to warrant full support? Maybe the "feminine" now symbolically resides with the Palestinians, even when terrorists in the Palestinian camp have undertaken sexual crimes. This could explain the strange silence from French feminists who seem ready to abandon the raped Israelis. The leader of the Marche des femmes, Linda Sarsour, already emphatically announced back in 2017 that "You can't be a Zionist and a feminist at the same time." Of course! Makes sense: Jews of all genders were for centuries symbolically feminine even when they were men. Now they've become male even when they're completely female. Do you follow me? That's why in the pro-Palestinian protests, the flags of the militant feminists and LGBT supporters can be seen: they find excuses wherever they can for the sexual violence and the homophobia of Hamas. Isn't all war in the first instance a war of the sexes? And the convergence of struggles effectively cuts off speech.

The gender matrix and the discourse of domination: this is the unfalsifiable and monolithic model that has imposed itself on many academics, intellectuals and thinkers who fill the campuses with it. In the battle of strong against week, of the powerful against the vulnerable, of the masculine against the feminine, the Jews now hold a dominant place. It doesn't matter if they're kidnapped babies, murdered men, or raped women. They will always be the masters of the situation. And not women. It's magic!

It's so magical that I, a Jewish woman, can almost imagine specifying my pronouns of choice, as it's sometimes recommended you do on American campuses. On my T-shirt from now on, I could wear a tag announcing my identity: "Hello, my name is Delphine. My pronouns are she/him." Because though I may talk about myself in the feminine, bizarrely the world has seriously masculinized me in its discourse. So I guess I need to adapt.

"But what about colonisation? The tragedy of the Palestinians? Isn't it time to recognize their suffering?" People shout at me as if I wasn't in agreement about that. But what is the link here? Does the suffering and injustice to which the Palestinians are subject and which demand reparation, does that make all Israelis without distinction, and by extension all Jews, powerful? Does it make the Hamas murderers of children and rapists of women, the incarnation of the so-called "weak" sex?

It makes no difference that for years I have been forcefully calling for the recognition of Palestinian rights, for a two-state solution. Because ultimately, it's precisely for the force with which I have been advocating that I will be blamed. That very force is once more the sign of Jewish power.

Accusing the Jews of wielding too much power is a constant in history. It is a fantasy that predates the arrival of the state of Israel, and the Six-day War of 1967 and its conquest of territory.

Jews are always perceived as those who have what others can't manage to acquire. If the Jews have a state or don't have one, if they're attacked because they have an army to defend them or because they don't, the accusation remains the same. As vulnerable as the next person, the Jew will always be perceived as stronger and luckier than others. That's how it is.

In days past, the Jew was a manipulative woman. Today, he's a dominating male. At root, what's the difference? A non-Jew will always show him that he's wrong. Hasn't he always actually wanted that which befalls him? Perhaps we can call this goy-splaining.

The only good news is that my television series—"Once upon a time . . . antisemitism"—is unlikely to end or be cancelled by the network or streamer. This infinite hatred will feed many more episodes. With the team of scriptwriters busy in my brain, we've already thought of next season. We told ourselves that with the terrible environmental crisis brewing, Jews will undoubtedly be accused of being its great promoters, of not recycling properly, or of polluting more than others.

And if tomorrow certain species of animals die out, Jews will more than likely be the guilty party. Imagine if zebras disappear? If that happens, it will be the fault of the Hebrews. Is the world in trouble? Moses must have something to do with that.

"Tell us mother, why is it starting again? Why is it always the Jews that are targeted?"

Questioned by my children, I would have liked to find the correct words. But fear made me mute. The day after October 7, a Sunday morning almost like all others, I said to my son, "Have you got nothing better to do than to watch this stupid stuff on the networks? Why don't you pick up a book instead!"

He shrugged and said, "Don't worry, I'm going off to play football."

A little while later, he sent me a little video, filmed by one of his friends in the stadium. On it you could see my son make a very skilful pass, shoot into the top corner, and score a goal. I clearly heard his friends applauding and congratulating him. But only one thing on the screen really drew my attention. Not his kick, nor the goalee who let it through . . . but a little thing that twirled near his face. At the end of a golden chain, his star of David had come out of his T-shirt and was dancing in the air to the rhythm of his movements on the field. I felt a familiar fear rise in me, something that probably came from the depths of time, perhaps pre-history, or antiquity. It's a fear that had surely passed through the Renaissance, even through the French Revolution, to end up stuck in my throat, making my body in October 2023.

My son came home a little later. I turned to him and said:

"You know what would be best? If you took off your star of David. Yes, I'd like you to do that, just for a few days, or weeks, just the length of time it takes for things to calm down. You will, won't you?"

My son came up to me softly and took me in his arms. He whispered into my ear: "No way, mom! I'm keeping it on."

My child taught me one of those lessons that, throughout history, runs backwards—the lesson that a son gives his mother, or that each new generation offers the preceding one when it stands up for itself. And I felt terrified, anxious, shaken, but incredibly proud.

"Once upon a time . . . the Jewish mothers . . ."

8
Conversation with Those Who Do Me Good

3:42. 4:53. 5:20 . . .

Night after night I try to remember at what times I look at the clock. For weeks now the ritual has been the same. Only the numbers vary.

Before October 7, I had never suffered from insomnia. I wasn't acquainted with that moment when the mind is agitated, when you put off looking at the clock for fear of the information it will communicate. I had been ignorant of this state of being, of those long minutes when the brain refuses to have visual confirmation of what it already knows intuitively: dawn is still far away.

Now, night after night, I discover an unknown world: sounds, movements, even looks. I have understood that I have long, without knowing it, been spied upon in my sleep. My cat spends his night on my bedside table, watching me.

Is he doing research on human nature? Is he keeping watch over me or, rather, observing me like a guard doing his rounds? I opt for the second option: my cat is the most anxious of animals, in a permanently suspicious state. I adopted him years ago, when he was already adult, from the RSPCA. I know nothing about his earlier life, but it evidently left him with a deep uneasiness. He communicates in no uncertain terms that I will never be worthy of his trust, neither I nor anyone else for that matter. My cat doesn't believe in humankind. I would love to prove him wrong, but nothing convinces him. And these days, I'm short on arguments. My cat is a lot like my Granny: he has seen too much. He mistrusts everything, and life has proved to him that abandonment is always lurking. So, he probably tells himself that he'll learn trust in another life.

When I adopted him, I suggested to my children a series of names for him, one more original or funnier than the next. I tried to persuade them to opt for "Bat Shalom,"simply because it tickled me to be able to introduce him as "my cat, Bat Shalom." Apparently, I was the only one who found this funny. The children shrugged with just a hint of condescension and opted, without consulting me, for a much more appropriate and banal cat name. These days I tell myself they were right. In our times, it's better to avoid names that are too Jewish.

At night, in the darkness, I see his eyes, like two translucent pearls, staring at me. My insomnia doesn't seem to surprise him. It may well be that my anxiety has sparked some empathy in him. Often, when I get up, he accompanies me in my nocturnal round. I sneak into the same dark places as he does. Sometimes I turn a lamp on to read a few lines. More often I listen to music. It's not usually instrumental. I need voices, preferably women's ones. They calm me. Barbra Streisand, or Barbara, the French cabaret singer who grew famous in the fifties and sixties. They murmur "Memory all alone in the moonlight" or "Cette petite cantate, fa, sol, do, fa . . ." "Papa, can you hear me?," "Mais les enfant ce sont les mêmes, à Paris ou à Gottingen." The singer-songwriter, Anne Sylvestre, often takes over. Her songs have been with me forever in my times of great sadness or in my quests for serenity. There's one song in particular: *Les gens qui doutent*—"People who doubt."

"*J'aime les gens qui tremblent, que parfois ils ne semblent capables de juger*
J'aime les gens qui passent moitié dans leurs godasses et moitié à côté."

"I like the people who tremble, for at times they seem incapable of judging
I like the people who spend half their life in their shoes and half next to them."

Several years ago, I even translated this song into Hebrew.[7] I wished that someone might take it up in Arabic and that these versions could be disseminated in the Middle East, where certitudes create so many victims, whether civilian or military. War has always followed this

[7] https://www.youtube.com/watch?v=Pqebibf8zRE

strategy: each camp makes doubt its principal target and seeks to bring it down by bombing the HQ of free expression. You need only look at television, the press and above all social media to be convinced of that. Nothing there to shake you in your convictions. Certainties ring out their little songs everywhere.

Anne Sylvestre's songs have always done me good, but it took me a long time to understand why. When I read her family history, some clues emerged.

I understood that this daughter of a wartime collaborator had turned her songs into a form of resistance against her origins. As if each phrase she wrote bore an undertone: I'm the child of a coward or a bastard, but I'll fight my way out of that legacy. That's perhaps why she wrote so many lyrics for children—nursery rhymes that teach you how to grow up and how to distrust, how to do up your shoelaces and how to trust. These little fables create marvellous possible futures for her and for us. Can you get past the past except by rewriting it?

For weeks now, I've been thinking a lot about what does me good and even more about those who do me good. Not only in the midst of this dark night of history, but in a more general way. I think of those who have always been my life rafts and springs of living water.

I realised just how much I needed to surround myself with people who know they're haunted. People who welcome in the ghosts of their history and allow them to speak through what they write, compose, sing, or make. I need to surround myself with those who know what they owe to their revenants and who don't pretend the past is altogether past.

Since October 7, certain friendly conversations have saved me from drowning. These dialogues are buoys and I hang on to them. Such were the conversations I had, for example, with Wajdi Mouawad. He is haunted by the Lebanese war. His ghosts took residence in his life during his childhood, at the moment that his family recognised that they would no longer be at home anywhere. This exile with no hope of return has been a part of his creative work ever since. Few people speak so compellingly about hauntings. Ghosts gnaw at everything he writes or puts on stage. It makes no difference if there is a single actor on the stage, or five or ten, the stage also contains a whole crowd of revenants, absent ones who line up behind those present and appear stage-side in the garden or the courtyard whenever it suits them.

In fact, they follow him everywhere, even when he's far from the theatre. Each time we meet somewhere, in a café or at home, I have the feeling that he hasn't come on his own. His invisible cohort follow him everywhere. And since mine is just as sticky as his and a whole host of "*dybbuk*" souls are constantly with me, there are far too many of us at the table. We may well be alone, he and I, but they outnumber us. They talk loudly and even with their mouths full. They cut off our speech for good and become parasites on all our conversations.

Just after October 7, we met at a café, all ten, or one hundred of us or more . . . We were visibly devastated by the situation and the lack of sleep meant we weren't in good form. So we talked about the hatred that disfigures us, and which is escalating here, there, and everywhere around the world. Right here, too, where we pretend we've buried it.

And that's when he told me that among all the other hatreds, he knew that there was one very particular, a kind of fundamental hatred, a detestation of Jews, which, from his point of view, is the mother of all the others. He told me that his parents had cultivated in him a great deal of love, tenderness, and affection, but that they had also sewn deep inside him the seeds of that particular poisoned plant. He knew that this vegetation was growing inside him, ready to burgeon and even produce terrifying fruit. But he added that he had decided to dry out that particular terrain: not to water, nor fertilise that swampy marsh. He would never allow those hideous weeds to grow.

What he said was so powerful and courageous, that it seemed to me all the ghosts at table with us, both mine and his, and even those who happened by chance to be passing by, grew silent. Their mouths were agape. They knew very well that even in their own times, when they were alive, they would never have been able to put it as well as he had. He had really pulled the rug from under their feet.

Thinking of the wisdom of this gardener of humanity, I remembered the most famous tree in the Bible, the one that grows in Genesis. Planted in the Garden of Eden, the "tree of knowledge of good and evil" reminds humans that death threatens them: death that strikes them down or the death of those they strike down.

"You must not eat from the tree of the knowledge of good and evil, for when you eat from it you will surely die." (Genesis 2:17)

This verse in French finishes with the words, "De mort tu mourras."—"Of death you will die." Apparently, one can die of things other than death.

Other conversations brought me forcefully back to life. The one I had a little while back with the Goncourt Prize-winning Algerian author and journalist Kamel Daoud was one such.

I've admired this man for a long time. But after October 7, when a dialogue between us was proposed, I jumped at the opportunity. Open dialogue in a time of war is a rare thing. To meet the other and find the gateways to that which might link us can almost become an impossible mission. The rules of war have always been the same: you attack the bridges and reinforce the walls. Today relations are such that you not only get rid of bridges but also their builders. We consolidate the fortress of one group or another. And in doing so, we reinforce our solitudes.

So, I went to the meeting with Kamel, just to assure myself that my drawbridge was still lowered and worked.

At the meeting, there were a lot of people. Not only the journalist who had brought us together, but also

1000 phantoms who had found it useful to make the journey so as not to leave us alone.

There were his from Algeria, mine from Eastern Europe, and those from the Middle East who always manage to take up more room than the others. I wondered in what language they would all be able to speak to one another, and if they too would engage in the victimhood stakes: "I've suffered more than you . . ." "No, I have . . ."

Kamel spoke first and he silenced them with peerless eloquence. The sorrows of a blood-soaked Algeria, the 200,000 dead of the Algerian civil war, or "the black decade" as those years are called, were certainly there. The ghosts reminded us that they were hardly talked about anymore. They don't interest many people. But what can one do? They don't live in the Middle East and it's not my fault, that they weren't killed by Jews!

(*Oy vey*! I shouldn't have said that. I think of all those who might read this line straight, blind to my irony, and I shudder. I tell myself to delete it. But Kamel would agree: to give up our subtext, ironies and dark humor would condemn us all. That kind of censorship will only enclose us further in the dungeons of identity.)

Kamel often quotes the celebrated Palestinian poet Mahmoud Darwish, who used to say to the Jews: "Do you know why we're celebrated, we Palestinians? Because you're our enemies [. . .] If we were at war with Pakistan, no one would have heard of us."

Kamel talked about the hatred of Jews and what it

means in the world into which he was born. "Do you know that where I grew up, we call every Arab who wants emancipation and freedom of thought, a Jew?"

I found this crazy, but at the same time full of hope for the antisemites. We live at a time when so few people aspire to free thinking and so many prefer to cling on to a readymade narrative prepared by their tribe or grouping, I told myself that with this definition of Jews, there would soon be very few of them in the world!

And that's when Kamel talked to me of the rhinoceros. Not about flora or gardens or dangerous plants, but of fauna, zoology, and that bestial propensity within all of us.

He reminded me of the Eugène Ionesco play, which I had completely forgotten. The one where a man notices that all the people around him are becoming rhinoceroses. He wonders whether he'll be able to resist his gregarious instinct, all the social pressure, and somehow remain the last Man. He wonders whether he'll be able to prevent "rhinoceritis" from swallowing up his liberty and his humanity.

"These days," Kamel said to me, "rhinoceritis is equivalent to our ambient antisemitism."

How to resist it when there's a rhino-horn growing on so many known faces, including those of friends and acquaintances—near ones who allow it to get bigger and pay no attention.

Listening to Kamel, I thought of Genesis once more and the beginning of the world in the Bible. On the sixth day of Creation, both animals and Man are made, in other words both the rhinoceros and humans. The reader must inevitably ask what separates the two. What differentiates one from the other, given that they're created at the same time? Aren't they both animals? Not at all, the Bible tells us: man is capable of doing one thing that the other living things can't do. He alone can name the world, express the parts of Creation. But to name things is to share in the responsibility for what they become. Without that work of language, we remain rhinoceroses. When words no longer have any sense, the world disfigures us.

Once more, the ghosts in our conversation went silent. They didn't need to shout and scream because a strong and very human voice promised them that they wouldn't be forgotten.

These last weeks, such conversations and many others have saved me. I feel deeply grateful to these just voices, these voices of the Just who have appeared in my life like benedictions. Literally—as voices who speak the good.

Their ability to see the threats clearly, to look at what is growing either in a garden or in a face: the seed planted one day by people we love, or the epidemic that deforms the words of those dear to us. In brief, their ability to track antisemitic discourse, in themselves, in their brothers or friends, has amazed me.

Of course, history tells us that no one has a monopoly

on hatred. The Arab or Muslim mind is no more a natural home for it than any other. Didn't it live very comfortably and for a very long time in the Christian mind?

I can't help thinking about its theological origin and what it was that made the Jew damned or detestable for so many Christian and Muslim thinkers.

One of the roots of this hatred is perhaps to be found in ideas about origin.

Once upon a time . . . that's how all tales and legendary narratives begin. Each narrates the beginnings of their history in their own way. But how complicated it is to accept that there was anything before us! How difficult it is to know or to acknowledge that there were other times—in all the senses of the word—before my own "Once upon a time!" How painful it is for a man or for a religion to come "after"! It isn't hard to understand this. It's akin to the pain of the younger child who asks throughout his life why his big brother was already there before his birth, or in his absence. It may seem trivial and almost naïve, but the problem of chronology haunts theology from its origins. All the theologies . . .

For centuries Christians affirmed that they were the "True Israel," God's beloved child, the one faithful to the original message, the one through whom the alliance would be made, the clauses of which had been renegotiated in a New Testament. They thus told themselves that the oldest son had been disinherited to the benefit of the more valiant younger one. The Jew, the first born, was perfidious and a deicide, had betrayed the ancestral promise. Blind to the truth, he no longer deserved the confidence of the divine. We had to wait for the Second Vatican Council of 1962 for another story to be written, a different "Once upon a time" for Christianity.

Muslims, too, had to consider their relationship to the point of origin, and notably to the influence of the Jewish tribes on their prophet. Mohammed had dreamed of some recognition from the children of Israel in the Peninsula, but it didn't materialize. Why do they so stubbornly resist acknowledging the arrival of a new messenger? Why do they refuse the greatness of this new religion? Some Muslim theologians affirm that the Bible was the truncated version of a single authentic text, the Koran. "Once upon a time . . . a lie," they say. And once more, a truth others have tried to falsify is announced, that of Islam.

Ever and again the question of the relationship to "the first beginning" repeats itself. It's well known: we always come back to our origins in the end. To what came before us, before our birth or our revelation.

But if there was someone before me, someone who must, therefore, inevitably have influenced me, do I owe him anything? No, no, I can't owe him anything. That would mean I'm indebted. And what's more exasperating than realizing you're in debt! On top of everything, that would entail the scandal of not being at the origin of yourself. The horror of not being "pure." If there really was someone who came before me, nothing is pure, certainly not the origin, the first beginning. And what's more exasperating than knowing you're indebted. Then there's the problem of not being at the origin of yourself. Now there's a real scandal! Worse . . . it's a horror. Because then, if there really was someone before me, nothing is pure, and certainly not the beginning.

Oy a broch! You can appreciate how this idea exasperates fundamentalists, and all those confused orthodoxies, for they are founded on a myth of purity: purity of the body, of practices, of customs, and above all of origins. Hide this "before me" so that I don't have to recognize it!

This is a feast for the psychoanalysts who see in all this an illustration of a fundamental and universal need: forever and again, to kill the father. Kill the one who comes before, kill the one to whom you are indebted, kill the one whose law has the gall to constrain you.

But what about those Jews? They too must come from somewhere. They too must have a debt they want to extinguish and a father they'd like to kill. Just like everyone else. No one engenders himself. So, to whom are the Jews indebted? Upon whom can they turn their rage at their impure origins?

That's easy: they just need to turn against those civilisations that came before and that influenced them along the way. Turn to those great cultures where we find traces, and influences. Judaism too has a debt. It is the child of its encounter with Chaldeans, Canaanites,

Persians, Sumerians, and many others. Judaism bears traces of their influence.

But what luck—all of those cultures have disappeared, or almost! They left vestiges but there are no living souls claiming to be their descendants. There is no official heir with whom to cohabit, or worse, dispute a will. It's much simpler to confront origins when those who might incarnate them have had the good taste to flee.

No such luck for Christians and Muslims: the Jews, well they're ever there. Not only everywhere, but they seem to be somehow indestructible . . . They're murdered in the millions, and still they come back, like they were in the beginning. It's exasperating. The ideal would of course be to wipe out every trace of them, to delete what has been so as not to owe them anything. But that takes a lot of work. Almost a miracle.

A little while back, on social media, I came across someone who really believed this was possible. On his profile, just before Christmas, this man emotionally saluted the millions in the world who were preparing to celebrate the birth of a Jewish child in Bethlehem, over two thousand years ago. In another post, devoted to the Israeli-Palestinian conflict, the same man said: "Everyone knows that there were no Jews on this land before 1948." A Christmas miracle: in this man's mind Jews could have been there and not have been there at the same time. They may have originated in this region, but they have no link to it.

"Dear Santa Claus,

This year, I've been very good. So, as a present, I'd like . . . a magically clean slate. I'd so like to be able to wipe out my inconsistencies and get rid of everything in History that bothers me. Write it over again in a way that works for me, and have it begin with me."

Maybe all of us wish this in our own way: to change the beginning of our history. Wipe out what came before and rethink the origins of the world . . . The point from which all fictions can be imagined.

I, too, think of all this when I'm doing battle with my insomnia . . .

4:28 A.M.: I grab my computer, open a browser, and type in "the origin of the world." Of course, an image comes straight up. I should have thought of this earlier. Right there, in all its indecency, is Courbet's famous painting of the origin of the world: it depicts a woman's half open vulva and her abdomen.

In my nocturnal delirium, I allow my thoughts to wander. What if in fact the root of the problem lies here? What if the real germ of antisemitic hatred was sown *there*. Less in the wish to kill the father than in hatred of the mother, the womb of the world. The will not to see the hole from which we originated, and so to forget that another was there before us, had perhaps loved, honoured, or profaned our origin, and that is in fact *why* we were born?

Do we reproach the Jews precisely for being a hole

in our conscience, one we want neither to see nor know? Reproach them for being a mystery we'd love to be able to stop looking at, exactly like Courbet's painting? Oh, this intolerable origin of the world!

In the beginning, the Bible says, humanity was created at the same time as animality, whether that of the rhinoceros or that of the cat. And humanity returns to that animality when it no longer knows how to "name" what is happening to it. This humanity may well know that in its garden there are dangerous trees that could very quickly produce evil and sow death, yet it often prefers to water the climbing plants of hatred and watch them cling onto frustrations.

In Genesis, the hate that dehumanises returns again and again. And even the words are repeated. For example, one of the recurring phrases, returning almost like a stutter, is about beginnings.

"There was evening, and there was morning—the first day . . . There was evening, and there was morning—the second day . . . There was evening, and there was morning—the third day . . ."

Each day of Creation is announced in this way. Evening, then morning.

From this simple repetitive statement, Jewish tradition draws a surprising law—that of the calendar. This states that the day never begins with dawn, but always in the evening with sunset. When light vanishes, we can think we are already tomorrow.

We all know this well, in reality: at the beginning, there is no clarity, but always obscurity, darkness. There is never what we can see, but only that which we can neither see nor know.

The world begins and begins again when we know what we owe to the night that precedes our birth. This is what the fundamentalists and those who hate ever refuse to accept. There was a night before their birth and the day had already begun before them. And that refusal of what has come before them is not without link to their hatred of the other, and especially of Jews, that black hole of their history.

At the heart of my night and my insomnia, I can't stop remembering. Since October 7, it's so dark. Yet in this darkness there are songs and there are people, there are voices and precious encounters. There are beings who were there before me in the night of my prehistory. I want to believe that with them, dawn will come more quickly.

9
Conversation with Israel

Left . . . Right . . . Left . . . A few weeks ago, I took up boxing. I would never have thought of myself doing that. It doesn't seem like me at all. I've always found it grotesque. Left . . . Right . . . Left . . . to punch someone in order to relax. As if there weren't enough violence in the world already without having to add one's personal release to it.

Yet here I am. My coach comes to the house twice a week. He knocks at the door, and I immediately switch off all my news feeds. I open the door to him, and I have the feeling that through my fists I've let go of all that my eyes have refused to absorb. I free myself from the images of war as I land a few punches. He corrects my jab and my hook. He tells to watch my posture, to think about my attack, not to forget my defence. I breathe, I sweat, and my heart races. Sometimes I burst out laughing, simply because of the gestures and terms he uses. In the context of war, these are like an inoffensive and distanced version of another reality that won't leave me. Attack, counterattack, pause, end of break . . . Left . . . Right . . . Left . . . I punch.

I think precisely of that, of the left and the right. Above all, of the left, which this situation has KO'd. Of its political inclinations which, for many of us, no longer make any sense, or seem to have lost the clear orientation they had. Before this, we knew how to situate ourselves in the ring of our engagements. We jumped about in our corner. It was our territory, our comfort zone. And now, it's over.

It's crazy how many of my friends on the left have become right-wingers. Not in their own eyes, but in those who observe them. They may not have moved a centimetre, but the carpet has moved beneath their feet and there's a crowd shouting at them: "Fascists, Conservatives, Reactionaries."

It's madness, too, how many personalities of the ultra-left sweep away, with a circular gesture, loyalty to their group, and absorb a discourse that could easily have been borrowed from the ultra-right, a discourse of identity-obsession or ethnic patronage.

Dodging is everywhere and language uses some mighty uppercuts. I, for instances, had the habit on social media of being seen as a "dirty lefty, too liberal, and without sufficient respect for tradition." I got used to it. But now I understand nothing. The referees must have changed, because suddenly I've become a "racist, a Zionist, complicit in genocide."

Sometimes I post messages, and I find myself "liked" by celebrities on the extreme right who, until recently, would rather have thrown me a left hook. Winning their gratitude and their support is extremely painful to me. Simultaneously, I'm dropped by my partners in age-old struggles, who from now on do everything they can to prevent "full contact" with me. It's very troubling.

When words no longer mean very much, better to end up saying any old thing, preferably with humor. The other day, for instance, we had just sat down at the table when I decided to give my children a lesson in all this, in the form of a three-point attack. It was a way of testing the rapidity of their reflexes. I said:

"My dears, I have three things to announce: your mother adores boxing; she is now a right-winger; and she certainly doesn't want you to go to Harvard."

We all burst into loud laughter. In this grotesque announcement, there was certainly one truth, but which one? None of us could say. The world had changed so much. As for us . . . well, not as much as all that.

French boxing, Thai boxing, English boxing . . . Various cultures have developed their own styles of combat. Bizarrely, for a long time, French Jews didn't take part in competitions. Neither punches, nor kicks: my ancestors must have learned to fight in different ways. Often, they accepted being the punching bag of others, the one who takes the blows without fighting back . . . or doing so by other means: adapting, moving quickly and far, escaping whether by mind or foot in order to carry on living elsewhere.

It's a little strange because the Bible provides many

models of struggle as sources of inspiration. You could begin with a man who was a champion in all categories of face-to-face combat. He could easily have been imitated. Genesis recounts his story in a famous episode.

There was once a child called Jacob, born into a family of biblical patriarchs in a promised land, but who had a lot of difficulties. Bad luck, he wasn't born alone. He had a twin called Esau with whom from the very start he had little in common.

Jacob has smooth skin. He's fragile, kind and rather feminine. He's his mother's favourite. She protects him because she senses he's vulnerable.

His brother Esau is covered in hair and it's red, as if he were wearing a coat of fur. He's strong and muscular and quickly becomes a talented and cruel hunter: an adventurous man who conquers territory without fear or hesitation.

The rivalry between the brothers grows. Jacob ends up escaping and living elsewhere, building a life far from his brother. But one day fate determines there must be a face-to-face encounter. Jacob knows he has to return home and see his brother. He has to confront his past. The Bible doesn't recount that he prepares for combat by running through snow or climbing mountains on the double like Rocky Balboa. But the Bible reader is aware that he is preparing for a confrontation. It isn't the one Jacob has been anticipating.

The most famous combat in biblical literature takes place that night on the banks of a river. Jacob is alone on the road when his opponent appears. Who is he? A man? An angel? A hallucination? His conscience? The text doesn't say, nor is where the question lies. Only the confrontation matters.

The struggle lasts a whole night. At dawn, exhausted, Jacob, who we imagined fragile and vulnerable, ends up winning. His opponent throws down his gloves—not, however, before wounding his adversary. It's an important wound, to the hip, and the rotation of his hip joint will never be the same. Jacob understands that he will no longer be able to walk fully straight. He will limp. He will have to pursue his route hobbled. And it's at this point that the being who confronts him, the loser in their match, offers him the strangest of gifts. It takes the form of a benediction: "From now on, you will no longer be called Jacob, but Israel[8] because you have struggled against God and you have won."

End of the encounter. The two boxers leave the ring. But the reader who has been attentive to the text leaves it knocked out, powerfully struck by a detail. The name Israel, the very name that obsesses so many today, who either hold it dear or despise it, comes from this moment. Israel in the Bible is not the name of a country or of a people. It is a man's name. It's the identity of a being who has fought, and who will forever bear the trace of that original combat.

The entire paradox of the episode lies in this strange utterance: the fragile child becomes the man capable of

[8] Israel comes from the Hebrew root "to do battle with God."

victory, not because his body is intact but because he knows himself damaged. While he is still Jacob, he is unharmed. It's when he triumphs, that he acquires a limp. Forever rendered fragile in his equilibrium, he now bears the name of the fighter.

Jacob's body is flawless and defenceless. That of Israel is wobbly but capable of responding to attacks.

The entirety of Jewish history, or almost, is contained in this combat between these two conditions and two identities. For millennia, the Jews were Jacob, fragile and vulnerable, at the mercy of all the Esaus of history who hunted and murdered them in the lands where they attempted to settle. Like Jacob, they were accused of trickery and deceit, of not being worthy of trust or of usurping it. They had to try to defend themselves by other means: by playing with words, alliances, forms of knowledge. They almost never boxed, that was not their style. In the "heavy weights on their shoulders" class, they never had a boxing ring in which they could plan their movements, or a referee who would arbitrate in their favour. Such were the deprivations of my people across their history, in so many places and periods. First round, second round, and so it went on.

In 1948, a country came into being based on the preposterous and shocking idea of a return match. A "never again" which would turn Jacob into an Israel in a state of becoming. His narrative would be that of a struggle not to vanquish but to survive. This is the sacred narrative of a Jewish self-governing state that has accompanied Zionism since the origin of the project. A different kind of Jew would have to live there, a being who knew how to use his hands and not just his mind and feet, a being who could plant his feet and box, farm the earth and return the blows aimed at him. This being would know how to find nobility again in boxing—that "noble art"—as well as in the others.

The history is well known. Some consider it caricatural or falsifying, qualifying the project as a usurping, colonialist one. They're free to forget History, that which was supposed to be a partition, or that could have been a peace accord.

But we know the story since then a little better.

On October 7, a strange phenomenon occurred. It seemed to many of us that the ancestral combat recounted in Genesis was being replayed, but backwards. Israel had become Jacob again and been plunged into a terrifying night.

Jacob had returned, not on the paths of the diaspora, which he knew well, but in the land of Israel, where he wasn't supposed to appear—the land that had promised to rid him of his impotence. This limping, wounded country, had not been protected by its military, or its economic power or strategic importance.

On that day, the Israeli started oddly to resemble a diaspora Jew. He bore the signs of pain and impotence. He limped as much as we did. *On October 7, Israel made its grand return into Jewish history.*

Fifteen days earlier, on the 24th of September, I was in Paris in front of my community on the solemn day of Yom Kippur. That day I delivered a sermon I had hesitated to write. The sermon spoke of Israel, and I knew the content would disturb some of the faithful: "Talking politics on Yom Kippur, what an odd idea? Do you really want to set the members of the community against each other?" I advanced in the way a boxer enters the ring, my stomach in knots and my fists at the ready. I spoke the words with a great deal of apprehension.

I find it difficult to reread the words now, so much are they haunted by a form of tragic premonition. That day, I spoke of the danger that Israel runs into every time it feels infallible, each time it believes itself legitimately settled and in its land or certain of its rights, each time it forgets the features of the Other facing him. In this circumstance, Israel tramples on Jewish history and the lessons it has taught about vulnerability. In front of my entire community reunited on the most solemn day of the Jewish year, I pointed a finger at the current Israeli government, its arrogance and the hubris of power and might it cultivates in the voices of certain of its ministers. Their cult of the land and religious supremacy is, from my point of view, as far as possible from what Jewish wisdom has taught us. In fact, as if by chance, their party is called "Jewish power," as if these words can successfully cohabitate.

In my understanding, Judaism is never a matter of might. This doesn't mean that it is condemned to weakness, but rather that it is strong in its ability to invent itself again out of vulnerability. It proposes, as does Jacob who becomes Israel, to make of everything that is wobbly, and while leaning on weakness, a site of resilience and survival.

If Judaism doesn't act in this way, Jacob's struggle will inevitably have another outcome.

If Jacob doesn't become Israel, he becomes Esau, a man of force, who only knows might and lives only by that, a man who idolizes the land and forces its inhabitants to submit. Child of the diaspora that I am, heir to the limping Jacobs of history, I look at this country that I love, and I have qualms about its Esau-ification. I so want it to emerge from this night in a different way, transformed by its wound.

I am not naïve. I know perfectly well why it is obsessed with force. You would have to be ignorant both of history and psychology not to understand. The memory of the diasporic past and incessant wars with neighbours reinforced the quest for power year after year and turned the quest almost obsessive. Where once exile prohibited Jews from being strong, Israel now forbids them to be weak. The blows and the battles come, one after the other, like the political gyrations that land us where we swore never to go . . . Left . . . left . . . left . . . right . . . right . . . ultra-right. That nationalist and messianic upper cut.

Session after session, my coach repeats it to me. To win a match there is only one method. While fighting, you have to be able to alternate strong moments with weak. There are moments in which we can attack and knock our opponent down, and others when we accept that we have to step back in order to see how our opponent is fighting. We observe him. We allow him to advance. We give him room. He reveals himself, as within ourselves we prepare a counterattack. Strong moments and weak moments. I don't know if Israel, now at war, can hear the lesson of being faithful to Jacob and not turning into Esau.

Since October 7, the combat has grown. It's night in the world, like in the moment of confrontation in Genesis. And I don't know when dawn will come, nor if it will bring a benediction with it. I don't know what name the winner will bear, or even if he'll have one. What will he have learned from his might? Will he feel invincible? It would be the worst outcome. Where will he find the wisdom, from everything in him that knows itself broken, to construct a just society?

10
Conversation with the Messiah

For weeks now I've been trying to have a dialogue with a deaf pain. Deaf or very hard of hearing. Whatever the case, it doesn't respond to any of my calls. It ignores me and wants to know nothing of either my reasoning or my pleas. It remains inconsolable. I can talk to it very softly, sing it lullabies in Yiddish, try to make it laugh. Nothing works. I can try to rouse happy memories for it, the voices of beloved ghosts, caring friends who cajole, or envelop it with all the love of my children—nothing soothes it, and I am powerless to confront it. It cares not a jot for my words and pays no attention to my sign language.

On my side, I hear perfectly well. I hear those who say to me: "Get yourself together. Think of tomorrow." I also very distinctly hear those who invoke me and often ask, "What of the suffering of others? Do you only notice your own and ignore theirs? Have you no empathy for those on the other side?"

"On the other side". . . They make it sound like a confrontation between two sports teams in an international competition—as if it was a question, as a loyal supporter, of booing the adversaries, of defending the home team, of spitting on the other team's pain. I hate crowds and their murderous psychology.

I watch the images from the Middle East, the suffering on both sides. And, of course, my own suffering is fed by all this despair: the unending grief of the Israelis, the sobs of Palestinian mothers, all these broken lives whose stories will need to be told one by one. There are certain bastards who would like to force us into partial deafness, depending on our context and our selective memories or debts to identity. You're meant only to hear the screaming voices on one side, not the other. Either from the kibbutzim of the Negev and the grieving Israeli families, or from the ruins of Gaza and the villages of the West Bank.

I am invited (sometimes *summoned*) to speak of the fate of the Palestinians, as if the weeping for "my own" inevitably entailed my dehumanisation towards people on the other side.

"Go on, say that it's horrible. Say it. Louder! More publicly!"

I try time and again to find the right words, the right tone. I start to write or speak of what is evident—"It's horrible!"—and I see very quickly that my language is leading me down the wrong path and is about to strangle me. It doesn't know where to go next. Because the conclusion of my interlocutor is more precise and more accusing. What is expected of me, when I am summoned to speak, is never simply to voice my emotion or my pain, but always for me to launch an appeal. I am summoned in order in turn to summon a third party to act: the Jews or the Arabs, the UN, the World, God, the Pope, the Red Cross. Without simultaneously levelling an accusation and call to action, to simply speak the horror is never enough.

And suddenly my speech is—take your pick—guilt-ridden, stupid, or cowardly. On the one side there are the "informed" words of those who contextualise, who explain the tragedy, its historic sources, its moral necessity.

The voices of the more or less well intentioned arise as well and call for a ceasefire, and nothing else. As if that were enough. As if tomorrow didn't exist and that we wouldn't have simultaneously to answer for all the civilians who would need to be protected in the future.

A ceasefire, of course that sounds simple: who wouldn't want the fire to cease immediately and for peace to arrive as of now. Unless you're an extremist, you can't but commend the *a priori* evidence . . . Except if it leads to an impasse where other questions of life and death are concerned. For example: how to ensure that Israelis will be protected tomorrow against any further attack from Hamas, which it has vowed it will undertake. How to protect Palestinians from an Islamist leadership that will always prevent them from achieving freedom? How to free Palestine from those who instrumentalise it and render it violent while claiming they are defending it? How to save Israel from a government in a state of political and moral rot, which perceives itself as faithful to Judaism and the only legitimate government?

How to "cease fire" in the minds of pyromaniacs? How to arm oneself against those over there and even here thousands of miles away who constantly torpedo the hope of peace by terrorising the future?

Like so many others, I search for the words which would really convey to both the Palestinians *and* the Israelis that their suffering will never leave me indifferent, that one has to cry with one side *and* with the other.

But war murders language and nuance as well as innocent people. Moderation grows mute, while extremism shouts at full volume. Slogans are bellowed out and measured positions are taken hostage.

Since October 7, I have sought to find these positions again, but language fails. Language contains "buts" that nourish the pain of both sides.

"On October 7 ignoble acts were committed, *but* . . ."
"Jewish women were raped, *but* . . ."
"The fate of the children of Gaza is terrible, *but* . . ."
"Innocents have been used as human shields, *but* . . ."

I vomit out all these "buts" which trample the responsibilities of one side and the other, and which murder our humanity. I would like to eradicate them in simple legitimate defiance.

I then hear the voice of my grandfather, the grammarian, ordering me to recite time and again the elementary school lessons.

"My big little granddaughter, remember that 'but' is a

coordinating conjunction. In order to remember, all you need to do is to name all of them: mais, ou, et, donc, or, ni, car. It's simple and memorable and all French schoolchildren learn it by heart: *Mais ou est donc Ornicar*? But where then is Ornicar?"

"It's not as simple as that. Gramps . . . You'd still need to know who this Ornicar is, and where he's hiding. I don't think I've ever come across him."

"Well, then, you'll just have to invent him: tell yourself it's a pseudonym, the name of someone good, a friend, an acquaintance, a visitor who you're waiting for impatiently. Go on! Try! Try to answer. So, tell me, my big little granddaughter, where then is Ornicar? Shouldn't he already have been here for some time, now?"

I listen to my Gramps and I obey, as always. This is how I now name my hope, my dream of peace. I imagine it hiding somewhere. So very well hidden, that it remains unfindable. From epoch to epoch, after all, we're always waiting for Ornicar, just as we wait for Godot. The stage set changes, the theatre moves, but we continue the search. We render it even more unfindable each time we put some "buts" in our sentences, each time we can't manage to cry for the grief of another and simply stay by his side. Each time we can't let go of the context long enough for a full moment of empathy with another human.

But where then is Ornicar?

We wait for him in exactly the way we wait for the Messiah: by carefully putting in place the conditions for his non-arrival.

"But . . . but . . . but . . . is he going to come? Maybe yes, maybe no."

And the more we talk of him, the smaller the chances of seeing him appear.

Suddenly, he's monopolising our conversations. His name doesn't ring out as much in these last years as it used to. Messianism here, Messianism there. Eschatological discourses are everywhere around us: the fanatics of the three monotheistic religions noisily echo each other.

Each in their own way wants to hasten the end of the world. There are the evangelical Christians who support Israel in order to hasten the arrival of Gog and Magog, the ultimate battle, and the return of the Saviour. There are the ultra-nationalist Jews, persuaded that they are carrying out the divine will each time they place a new settlement on the map. There they are, ready to reconstruct the Temple of Jerusalem and there to sacrifice cows and sheep and perhaps the entire world. There is radical Islam and its dreams of global conquest, the return of the legendary Caliphate, its passion for martyrs and love of stones which, according to the prophecy, will speak one day and say: "Look, a Jew is hiding behind me. Come and kill him."

The show promises to be spectacular. Ask for the program!

And all of them threaten to set fire to the world and spill blood in the name of their holy texts and beliefs. No matter that they can be read and interpreted differently.

They choose to transform all confrontation into religious war, to hasten the end of history in the name of their deadly readings. They're eager to play the game of "who will bring the catastrophe on us first" and they throw challenges at each other—like in the children's rhymes: "I hold you, you hold me, by the goatee. The first of us to die will face a machete."

Ornicar isn't prepared to come out of hiding for that. Those who pray for his coming are clearly those who most efficiently keep him away.

Franz Kafka, who has leant his name to an adjective that fairly accurately describes what we are living through today, understood it all too well. He said: "The Messiah will come on the day after his arrival. It's clear, the Saviour will only come when we no longer need him. Prior to that, we'll have to resolve our problems, so that he can appear. Humanity will find a way of improving its lot, and precisely because it no longer needs any external intervention, He will come."

"You no longer need me? Peek-a-boo, here I am!"

Before that, I fear he'll remain hidden or at least ultra-discreet, stashed in a name the meaning of which the many who invoke him are ignorant. "Messiah" is a biblical term. In Hebrew it signifies "*oint*" (messiah) which means oily, because that was how heroes in those ancient days were consecrated. A little oil was poured on their heads to signify their separate status. It's well known that oil doesn't mix with anything else. It floats above the rest.

In the Jewish tradition, the sages aren't satisfied with this oiled image. So they give the word another significance, much more digestible and talkable about in my sense of things. "Messiah" also means in Hebrew "to be in conversation." So the Messiah is someone who knows how to take part in, or perhaps is even the one who awaits, this conversation—the one who will come only when it takes place. Without talking to one another, no redemption is possible.

And what if this is precisely the challenge before us today: the challenge of relaunching the conversation? Finding the route to a conversation which could save us, a dialogue that war, fear, and certainties have interrupted.

For some time now, I have understood how difficult the conversation that I try to have with people, that takes place in my head and to which this book tries to give witness is.

Since October 7, it's as if our language is no longer able to speak. It constantly betrays us or turns against us. The words we considered penetrating lead nowhere, and those we thought mild soothe no one. Images, which can always be caricatured and manipulated, have replaced words on our screens. Our eyes, subjugated in this way, stupefy our ears and brain.

To talk in wartime is almost an impossible mission.

Talking, after the war, is almost as difficult. I am well placed to know that being the child of a family where speech was never completely found again, where lullabies, grammar and humor tried to cover over the silences.

So, I ask myself how might we invent another language, one with which to ask "How are you not? How isn't it going?" Learn to say that to one another and not only on one side of the divide. I adhere to past generations and their earlier efforts to use words to rise from the catastrophes we lived through.

I think of the novelist Georges Perec, who wrote *A Void*, a whole book without the letter "e." He wanted us to understand that without the sound of that "e," which in French is also "eux," or them, the lost ones, we would no longer be able to speak or read in the same way.

I think of Romain Gary who invented so many pseudonyms and identities to tell himself and us that he would never again be himself.

I think of Stefan Zweig, who preferred to die than witness a world in which words could not ensure our survival.

It's my turn to ask myself how to save words and save ourselves from what hatred does to all.

"*Oyvey.*"

In my family, conversation still often starts like that. An adult, a parent or a grandparent, comes into a room and repeats the old ancestral plaint. I suddenly wonder whether we're aware that in this expression which is integral to all the dramas of our history, a strange code lies hidden. Yiddish lamentation has always given shelter to the most sacred name of all. It's plonked there discreetly, neither seen nor known and it's the anagram of that ineffable Name, the name of the God whom Jews refuse to speak and others call "YEOVA, Jehovah, or Yahveh."

Oy veh. Yehova, but a mess . . . It's as if this profane expression of our pain always also hid a theological or political lesson. Catastrophe tells us, literally, of the toppling of the divine—a divine reversal. The letters get mixed together, words lose their sense, even the most sacred. And tragedy arrives.

In Yiddish, the complaint always speaks of the toppling of the world to which we are witness. What we thought sacred crumbles, and nothing makes sense anymore. By rearranging a few letters, praise is eclipsed and the monstrous appears.

This is how the ugliness of the world is always exposed: it attacks language first and massacres it. Beauty disappears in men's words and then in their world.

I don't know where the Messiah will come from and whether he has any reason to come. It seems to me he will be neither a minister, nor a general, nor a strategist. Perhaps he'll be a poet or an interpreter of scripture, a man or a woman who knows how to hear words, how to play with them and thus to build another world.

I opened this book with the words of a Palestinian poet, and I would like to close it with those of an Israeli poet. Both have been dead a long time, and I don't know whether they have met in any other context than the book you hold in your hands. If this book must serve only one purpose, I would like it to be that it permits their conversation or its pursuit.

One expressed himself in Arabic and the other in Hebrew. What's the difference! Both these words are (in Hebrew) perfect anagrams. Arabic and Hebrew: words written with precisely the same letters: *ayin-resh-beit-youd* and *ayin-beit-resh-youd*. They are the same intertwined word.

I'd like to think that Mahmoud Darwish and Yehuda Amichai are in conversation in these pages. In their words, there is no "but," nor is there any eternal hatred. There are the traces of the battles they fought and wars that were sometimes necessary. There is also an invitation to another kind of messianism. Not one that rushes us to the end of the world and leads us straight into apocalypse, but instead, one that says there is a future for those who think of the other, for those who engage in dialogue one with another, and with the humanity within them.

Once I was sitting on the steps near the gate at David's Citadel and I put down my two heavy baskets beside me. A group of tourists stood there around their guide, and I became their point of reference. "You see that man over there with the baskets? A little to the right of his head there's an arch from the Roman period. A little to the right of his head." "But he's moving, he's moving!" I said Redemption will come only when they are told, "Do you see that arch over there from the Roman period? It doesn't matter, but near it, a little to the left and then down a bit, there's a man who has just bought fruit and vegetables for his family."

From *Tourists* by Yehuda Amichai[9]

[9] *The Selected Poetry of Yehuda Amichai,* translated by Chanah Bloch and Stephen Mitchell. University of California Press, 1968

To think of another

To think of Humankind

To think of the heavy baskets that will need to be set down

For hope to be found again

Paris
14 December 2023
8th Chanukah Candle